ADVANCED SE
FOR BEGINNERS

For a complete list of Management Books 2000 titles,
visit our web-site on http://www.mb2000.com

ADVANCED SELLING FOR BEGINNERS

Alex McMillan

2000

Other Books By the Same Author
Your Ticket To Success
Entrepreneur

First published in 2003 by Management Books 2000 Ltd
Forge House, Limes Road
Kemble, Cirencester
Gloucestershire, GL7 6AD, UK
Tel: 0044 (0) 1285 771441/2
Fax: 0044 (0) 1285 771055
E-mail: m.b.2000@virgin.net
Web: www.mb2000.com

Printed and bound in Great Britain by Digital Books Logistics

British Library Cataloguing in Publication Data is available
ISBN 1-85252-426-X

Contents

Acknowledgements

I would like to thank the many entrepreneurs who have built profitable expanding businesses that have helped considerably with this work. I would also like to thank friends, loved ones, supporters, delegates on courses, business partners, employees, other authors and clients.

Specifically thanks to:

Rupinder Chana for his key input on sales techniques in each chapter

David Leyshon of Butler Recruitment (UK) Ltd

Richard Lowden of Eurodrive Car Rental Ltd

Sundry Sundaran of www.accountingcompany.co.uk for years of professional advice and expertise on entrepreneur issues

Kevin Uphill of Avondale Group Ltd

Alan Lowden for offering a considerable wealth of international commercial experience

Mark Hawkswell for being an expert sales professional model and advisor

David Maxwell of Peosys Ltd for innovations, ideas and being there

Chris King, Vijay Dhir and Richard Baxter for being interviewed

Tracy McMillan for constructive criticism

Louisa Carson for professional critique.

Dedication

To everyone all over the world with an entrepreneur dream.

Foreword

When Alex asked me to write the foreword for this book, I was naturally honoured. I would also wish the success and growth that I and my business have enjoyed, to others.

Alex was involved with my company from the beginning, over ten years ago. From the start, he offered us coaching, consultancy and training on selling.

Getting a business started from scratch is a challenge, to say the least. There are no established customers, no branding, head office or sales department, or even many staff to delegate to. Alex started with sales coaching from the time we opened our first branch and continued to offer group seminars as we opened more branches, now in all parts of the country. This foreword was written in a week when I had business trips to Spain, France, Jersey and Dubai. I am now living my initial dream. We rent cars in every continent of the world.

The path to growth has not been an easy one. There have been many obstacles and setbacks along the way. My staff and branches had to compete against extremely large, well-established competitors. My people therefore had to have sales skills that were significantly better than staff from those major businesses, with all their resources behind them.

Entrepreneurs have special development needs, quite different from when they were employees of large corporations. We thought big from the start and constantly looked for an edge over our competition. Entrepreneurs, though, do have advantages – passion, determination, willingness to work all hours and an obsession to be the best. This makes the way we sell and the way we present ourselves to our customers of paramount importance. Directors of small growth firms are in daily touch with their customers – use this advantage. This book will hone those skills, enabling you to get to the next growth stage.

If you have not set up on your own yet, do it – and persist on seeing your way through any obstacles rather than worrying about them.

If you are already in business for yourself, focus on increasing sales relative to costs.

At the end of the day, the prime importance for any entrepreneur is getting cash in regularly. This book will solve that one for you. I have applied many of Alex's lessons in achieving my success – they work.

Oh, by the way – did I mention we rent cars?

Richard Lowden
Managing Director
www.eurodrive.com

1

Introduction –
Advanced Selling for Beginners

Short-cuts for entrepreneurs

'Only those who dare to fail greatly can ever achieve greatly.'
Robert F. Kennedy

'If you do things well, do them better. Be daring, be first, be different, be just.'
Anita Roddick

'You can have brilliant ideas, but if you can't get them across, your ideas won't get you anywhere.'
Lee Iacocca

For those wanting to get straight to sales skills, there is a summary of key points at the end of this chapter.

This chapter ...
A   **Beginners?**
B   **Why 'for beginners'?**
C   **What is 'selling'?**
D   **Why 'advanced'?**
E   **The psychology of success**
F   **Other benefits of sales skills to entrepreneurs**

A – Beginners?

In the film 'The Matrix', the hero, who is under time pressure, directly downloads software straight into his brain making him a black belt within minutes. With this skill, he and others then go forth and achieve their objectives. That was my target in writing this book – to give **entrepreneurs** and other **non-sales professionals** selling skills in the shortest possible time.

I have an advantage on our above hero. Most of the 'software' for selling (learning, skills, techniques) is in fact already there, but filed for use under other applications. Using resources in a different way is at the heart of entrepreneurship. Therefore the concept will be an appealing one that fits naturally.

For example, have you ever ...

- ... asked someone out on a date and been accepted?
- ... asked someone out on a date, been rejected and got over it and asked someone else?
- ... persuaded your mum, when you were a child, to buy you some sweets after several rejections?
- ... been so passionate about something that energy and motivation were in abundance?
- ... made a new friend?
- ... asked a complete stranger in the street directions to somewhere?
- ... been determined to achieve something someone said you could not do?
- ... helped others?
- ... thought about a situation from the other person's viewpoint

The list goes on, and if you can say yes to most of the above, this book will develop your selling skill to advanced level in a very short time.

If you look at the various skills of sales you will soon realise that you not only have done it before, but you have done it before very well and many times.

Progress now:

Add one of your own examples to mine in the following list of sales skills:

a) **Cold approaches to strangers**
   - ✓ Asked someone in the street for the time or directions somewhere.

   ✓

b) **Pitched for the Business /Persuasion**
   - ✓ Asked someone for a date. Got your friends to play a sport with you.

   ✓

c) **Persistence**
   - ✓ Never giving up as a child, repeatedly asking for something from mum or dad.

   ✓

d) **Patience**
   - ✓ Waited in a queue for a long period of time. Sat and waited on a cross-Atlantic flight.

   ✓

e) **Motivation**
   - ✓ Arose early on a cold winter's morning to do something that needed doing.

   ✓

---

f) Determination
    ✓ Sticking through three years at college to get that degree.

    ✓

g) Written Communication
    ✓ Winning that interview for a job against fierce competition.

    ✓

So you have much more ability and practice at selling than you realised. You now need to take those skills, polish them up a little and apply them to selling.

B – Why 'for beginners'?

Having been involved in sales training for over ten years, I have learnt that the biggest demand for sales skills is actually from people not directly involved in sales. Therefore I have written this book for the specific needs of that group. A group which mainly consists of entrepreneurs of various types. A group that has its expertise elsewhere and are beginners in terms of not having attended courses, or been employed in a sales function.

The advantage in being beginners is that learning can progress far more quickly. This is because the novice does not have bad habits to de-learn, negative beliefs to be changed, or opinions to be defended. The beginner is by nature open-minded and receptive to new ideas. Like everything else in this fast changing world, methods of selling are moving on. The beginner has a better starting point from which to begin.

Sales I define as closing a deal for a product or service that you offer, in return for money (or other commodity). In business, there are many people that have to sell, whether they like to or not. People who set up on their own or run a small company do not have the resources to delegate to a sales department. In larger entrepreneurial concerns that do have established departments, the original entrepreneur will still have to sell. People such as Richard Branson and Bill Gates have clearly shown that they have learnt how to sell and still do it successfully. Like them, you may find that your need for sales skills is in addressing a small or large group. It is also important for entrepreneurs to understand the principles of sales for all their communication to the outside world.

I have spent the last twenty years focused on being an entrepreneur, and helping other entrepreneurs. This includes consulting and coaching, from small firms to companies that have become quite sizeable where the entrepreneur as the founder is the person the major customers want to meet. Business owners have to do the selling in addition to everything else that they do. Today, the number of people working for themselves is exploding.

As entrepreneurs have too much to do, you will be happy to learn that the book is designed for speed, practicality and rapid absorption.

C – What is 'selling'?

This book is focused on advanced practical selling techniques that can be learnt by entrepreneurs, quickly. This includes crucial areas such as confidence building and motivation. Many people in business, especially entrepreneurs, sole traders and consultants find that they have to sell and therefore need to gain skills that produce results fast.

This book avoids dependence on experience learning as it is based on that of top sales performers. If your main personal work is something other than selling, then you are unlikely to have the time to go through the basics and then build upon this through experience.

Sales books and training often have formulae for sales success that they claim will work on any prospect. In my opinion, based upon observation, they are as effective as all those diet books out there. I have found that top sales performers treat every person as a unique human being. They listen first and then are flexible in their responses, reflecting the needs and signals of that specific prospective client. Once you decide to focus on listening, business will increasingly come your way. Listening is relatively easy, you just need to make sure you are not filtering according to what you want or expect to hear. Much of this book covers the things to listen for.

I have read many books on sales and attended numerous courses. The emphasis has been on 'professional selling', which means looking after the customer's needs. To me the words that they use – 'Prospect', 'Cold Call', 'Pitching', 'Closing', 'Objection Handling', 'Sales Representative', 'Win Win negotiation' – do not suggest that the customer or potential customer's needs are being put first. 'Win Win', can suggest that there is an Us/Them contest going on. The important principle intended behind the expression is that both parties benefit. Yet the belief that selling is a contest has dominated sales training for years – there has been no new thinking or approaches.

Robert Seller
Sales Representative

The Selling Company Ltd
www.thesellingcompanyltd.co.uk

When somebody gives you a business card that says 'Sales Representative', what does that imply? To me it implies that their only objective is to procure sales for their company and earn commission. Nothing wrong with that, but when I buy from somebody, I choose people that convince me that my interests are high in their priorities, or that they have belief in what they are selling.

In my experience, people not in sales often see it just as the art of getting someone to buy what you offer. They conclude from this that in order to sell, you must be hard and pushy with the 'gift of the gab'. If you focus more on making someone else happy, you will receive better responses and spend more time listening than talking. You will also find that your own motivation is higher because your conscience is not wrestling with the ethics of what you are doing. Long term successful selling comes through understanding, helping and clarity of communication

I prefer people that demonstrate a real pride in their job, not a hard-boiled motivation to make money. I once went on vacation in Texas and was incredibly impressed at the level of service. I have a family of five and eating in a restaurant, for example, can be hard work. How refreshing to have service where the staff pre-empt any of your needs and cater (pardon the pun) to it with pride in their work. Does the following sound familiar to you? You spend a fair part of your time in a restaurant trying to get the attention of the staff to get served and chasing after them. In Texas, I tipped generously and although it's a long way, I will be back.

Selling is first and foremost about having a pride, a passion and a belief in what you are offering. If you have not got that, find something that gives it to you.

Try a business card that says something like 'Customer Satisfaction Director', and live up to it. Believe me, you will have a lot more happy customers that remember you. It will also set you up with a better mental attitude. Next time you are being 'sold' to, think how much it excites and motivates you that you are a prospect who has been cold called and closed on! This book will help you get into your customer's shoes and see selling from their point of view.

Robert Seller
Customer Satisfaction Director
The Selling Company Ltd
www.thesellingcompanyltd.co.uk

Most customers have become very weary and resistant to traditional mechanistic selling methods. Coupled with this are the advances in technology, meaning that the emphasis is more on listening, thinking and reacting appropriately than it has been in the past. Customers might not have a clear idea of their own needs and the solution can be creative. If you can think of a new way to satisfy their needs, there will be no competition. A new age is upon us, with abundant opportunities for entrepreneurs who thrive on change. The emphasis for this new age from a selling perspective is on *rapport, trust and listening* (When was the last time you experienced a sales representative take that approach with you?).

Every day, more than US$1 billion changes hands in New York alone. People like spending money, which is why they work so hard for it. Selling is not difficult. Often people do things that stop customers buying, such as ignoring them, talking rather than listening, asking the wrong questions and so on. All they often need is to stop doing certain actions. All you need to do is apply half of the principles in this book and you will outperform hard-boiled sales professionals with years of experience behind them. Yes, really, I have proved just that many times.

My belief (based on what I found by studying top sales professionals instead of designing theories) is that the emphasis has to be on 'opening' sales opportunities and then building relationships (as opposed to closing). By studying this book, you can bypass and avoid mistakes that are holding back many experienced sales professionals. To me, the term 'closing' suggests a door which is being shut to lock the customer into the deal. For business in the 2000s, we need to think in terms of finding 'keys' to let future customers in. We need to get that door wide open and keep it open. We need to change our thinking to see opportunities that were not open to us previously. I know that most future (potential) customers want to be present

customers and what we are doing or saying is somehow stopping them, putting them off. The challenge of professional selling is finding out (searching for the key to the door) what you can say or do differently to let them in as customers.

In summary, sales success comes from:

1. listening and observing to find a market that you can sell to
2. communicating well with yourself to produce a clear plan, consistent motivation and self belief
3. listening to prospective customers
4. being creative to exploit sales opportunities cost and time effectively
5. taking appropriate action and loving your work
6. banking the cash
7. keeping in touch.

D – Why 'advanced'?

The book assumes no previous knowledge of selling and goes straight to the techniques that top sales professionals use. Rather than learning by experience, this book contains what top sales performers do to get their results. It is based on my personal experience of over ten years of sales training and coaching and research in the area, coupled with the findings of NLP (Neuro Linguistic Programming – The Psychology of Success). In this regard, much of what first appeared in *'Your Ticket To Success'* is repeated and developed here.

It does, however, require some practice in the various techniques. Practice provides you with your own feedback and thus refinement of the effect of these techniques. This in turn will change your perception as to what you can achieve and your confidence level will rise. You will develop habits and automatic competence in applying the techniques. After applying the ideas in the following chapters, you will start to appreciate that you do not need to be born with the gift of the gab in order to excel in your commercial communications with others.

There is a common misconception I have found, that learning, by it's very nature, takes a long time. Actually it doesn't, nor does it take any great intelligence or other talent. All of us have sophisticated skills that we learnt in a short space of time. Non-swimmers fall into rivers and find they learn really quickly! People go to foreign countries and pick up a language in days, which they struggled with for years at school, coming to the belief they had no language ability.

The ideas in this book utilise and develop knowledge from a diverse cross-section of areas. NLP, the now established psychology of achievement, has contributed a great deal. However most of the material presently available on this subject is in a raw form, full of academic jargon, and needs to be interpreted in order to be of practical use to time-starved entrepreneurs. I have also avoided 'explanations of why' and concentrate on the practical usage of techniques instead. If you are the sort of person who likes to boast how many techniques you know or to show off the latest buzzwords, then look elsewhere. If, on the other hand, you want to transform your communication and influencing skills, magnifying your results fast, read on.

You have to think about marketing, which should always come before selling activity. Marketing is getting the phone to ring, selling is closing a deal when it does. Whatever you offer, you can probably now offer it worldwide without major investment. You need to stop thinking locally or at least redefine what local is. Let us say you are a one-man band consultant specialising in team building courses for companies. Ten years ago you would have visited the office of a local company and perhaps coached and ran courses for their staff to work better together. Today that same company has its team in various locations. Some of those locations are homeworkers. Thus their team identity, strength and co-operation has been significantly changed. The nature of their jobs has also moved on. Staff who used to make phone calls are now on the Internet or emailing for half of each day.

So, if for example, you are a provider of team building courses, you have got to move with the times. If you have a set of standard courses on offer, they need updating and new ones developed. You might be better off producing products such as DVDs, or blend new technology with old fashioned methods, so as to reach people in remote locations. Many will see these changes as a threat, but actually, in the above example, the team building need is far more important and challenging to the client than it was before.

I believe that traditional selling techniques themselves, with the emphasis on closing, have got to move on to maintain value. They do not offer enough to get ahead in today's faster moving, and constantly changing environment. Fortunately, most people selling and most companies for that matter are not moving forward fast enough. This means a wealth of opportunities for those that do. So this book advances you by avoiding a lot of time you could have wasted learning obsolete methodologies. Businesses large and small are fundamentally changing the way that they operate. As such, the way you are going to sell your wares has to constantly change to keep pace. A business executive who used to travel 60,000 miles a year has been replaced by video conferencing, Internet downloads and e-mail. Buyers have evolved, and become more knowledgeable and very sophisticated. Access to a world-wide market also means the world has access to yours.

We need to respond to varied communication and thinking patterns. Those who learn and apply the lessons in this work, will accelerate the value of their businesses. If you learn, apply, practise and master the ideas that follow you will find that your ability to develop rapport, listen, understand, be flexible and influence will be better than you currently believe possible. This belief change in itself will empower you to greater performance. Suspend scepticism, try it out and see the results. Dismiss this challenge and you will come second to those that take it!

Influence

People are happy to be influenced if it improves their situation. Before we can really master the influencing of others it is important to understand how we ourselves are influenced by others, in situations that improve or limit our lives. Where have all your influences come from? How did you form your opinions, values and beliefs about anything? How are they different from those of other people you know? How did they come to be influenced differently? When you are influenced, you are usually accepting the lead from somebody else because they gained a rapport with you. They have communicated or explained their position to you in a way you can understand and appreciate. They lead by example.

When running training sessions, one rather straightforward exercise I often finish with is as follows: 'In groups, over the next ten minutes decide on a meal out that you will all go to following the course.' Then I stand back and observe. Immediately, all group members are clearly influencing each other, in a variety of ways, even if they remain silent. Are they going to elect a leader? If so, who will pitch for it and who will manoeuvre to avoid it? Who is being led? Who has set clear objectives? When you have observed a straightforward decision like this and observed the patterns of influence, you start to appreciate more and more why coming to complex and important business decisions is a more complicated process than it first appears. Selling your ideas to others requires mastery at communication. This book shows you through the maze with tremendous short cuts, avoiding the need to learn by long and painful experience, which can itself lead to wrong or limiting conclusions.

Influencing forces which cannot be stopped are at work all the time. The important thing is to take control and harness these forces to ensure clear rapport and communication, thus leading to adding value. Have you ever been in a situation where you have communicated something with good intent to somebody and they have reacted negatively, despite your (to you) good intention? Perhaps finished by saying, 'What did I say?' After studying this book, you will be able to accurately predict the response to your communications, taking control of your desired outcomes.

To the person who is ready to take that challenge, welcome to what you will look back on as being the first day of the transformation of your business.

Some principles of psychology

Let us now look at some basic principles of psychology that set a foundation for the chapters that follow. All human memory is a distortion of experience, an internal representation of an event. Our conscious mind finds repetition boring, yet our unconscious mind, which makes most purchase decisions, thrives on it. Look at the success of McDonald's – same limited menu choice, same prices, seating and layout in all their worldwide operations.

We all perceive a situation differently. If you hold a meeting in your business and I asked the same ten participants later what transpired, guess what? I would have ten different versions of what happened. Each will be totally convinced theirs is the only version. Why is this? Well, we filter reality through what basically boils down to three distinct processes, *generalisation, deletion* and *distortion*. Our brain does this automatically. It generalises and deletes to cut down the sheer volume of information coming to us. Perceptions of events are like fingerprints, different for everyone.

Can you describe to me the details of all the cars you passed on your way to work this morning? At any instant of the journey can you describe in detail all the sights and sounds of everything going on around you. No, in fact we filter out more than 99% of the detail around us to stop our brains being overwhelmed, by concentrating on what has meaning for us. Distortion is the interesting one. What happens here, is that we compare new information and experience unconsciously to all our previous experiences. These previous experiences will have created habits, opinions, values and beliefs. We then distort the new information to fit into our reference frame. This is how we make meaning of new events. Let us have a look at the three processes in a practical example.

> Steve, a friend of mine, recently went to New York to raise finance for a new venture. He got out of the airport and hailed a cab. When he got out, the driver swore at him for not leaving a tip. When he got to his meeting, he retold his story. His colleagues said that their cab rides had been fine. On returning to the UK, Jonathan, a friend of his, was due to leave for New York and asked for any pointers.
>
> 'Whatever you do, don't travel by cab. The cab drivers are rude (generalisation), and they drive recklessly (distortion).' He did not mention that all his colleagues had no problems with the cab drivers (deletion). What is worse, Steve now has this story in his (unconscious) mind as a reference piece of information.

Do you see how important all this is for commercial communication? Everything anybody (a customer) has been previously told will have been 'filtered' in this way. The total picture it makes up will be reality for her or him. Saying any different will just conflict with what he or she knows to be true for their 'model of how the world goes around'. So the first essential thing to be aware of is that you are selling to their reality, not yours or anybody else's. The second important thing is to be able to reach that prospect in a way that makes sense to them.

The chapters that follow show you how to talk to someone with total respect for their 'model of the world', without the need for substantial knowledge of that person. It is in fact easier to achieve than you might imagine, and the results you get will impress you. You do not need any information other than what they give you in conversation. This book in essence is all about how we can reach the recipient of your communication in his world. That to me is the difference between professional communication and learning techniques by repeating 'parrot fashion'.

Remember that customers, and staff for that matter, believe that their model of the world is the real one, and for them they will always be right. 'Reality leaves a lot to the imagination!'

This book is comprehensive and covers everything you need to know about selling. Take it a chapter at a time or even in smaller chunks. Applying one idea or tip will move your business forward. The format has also been designed to make the material easy to use for training events. If you have a specific challenge around selling, you can also search for solution through the index, chapter or sub headings to find solutions.

In short, read and apply the principles in this book and you will increase the quality and quantity of your business performance. This is my personal guarantee to you. There are too many business professionals out there who read books and 'know what to do'. Doing what you know is the key, apply your learnings, get some feedback, adapt them, and then make more money ...

E – The psychology of success

I would like to include a brief background to NLP as it is relevant to this work. I first came across it myself in the early 1990s, later to progress through Practitioner, Master Practitioner and then Certified Trainer. In the UK, there is an association that runs two open conferences per annum. I occasionally present at these conferences and 'Advanced Selling for Beginners' was first run openly there to a group that were mostly entrepreneurs or independent consultants. I also run it as a 'webinar' – details of which can be found on **www.alexmcmillan.com**. Since its creation, NLP has continually grown in interest around the world. Wherever you are, there will be a local NLP organisation close to you.

In the early 1970s at the University of California, two men came together: Richard Bandler, a computer scientist, gestalt therapist and mathematician, and John Grinder, the Professor of Linguistics. Their plan was to model people who were making significant changes in others' behaviour. They initially studied three world class therapists: Fritz Perls, Virginia Satir and Milton Erickson. These therapists were at the top of their professions, creating dramatic and quick, yet long-term, change in their clients. From these extensive studies Bandler and Grinder produced a blueprint for peak performance. This model they called Neuro Linguistic Programming (NLP).

NLP is essentially a model of excellence and achievement of 'what works best'. It offers a systematic way of consistently achieving outstanding results across a broad spectrum of communication.

NLP is the answer to the question, 'What is it that makes the difference between somebody who is merely competent at any given skill, and somebody who excels at the same skill?' This question has led to a whole new understanding that has revolutionised the field of psychology, and hence selling – how we perceive the world and how we organise our thinking, feeling, skills and behaviour. NLP is still evolving, and is the subject of continuing innovation, development and exploding worldwide interest. It can be used remedially, so that, for example, if someone is not getting what they want out of life, it can allow them to uncover, change or transform what is holding them back. It can also be used to enable them to make enhancements, i.e. to achieve excellence in something they already perform well, often when they believed they had already reached the limit of their ability.

NLP involves the gathering of information to make models, based on the internal, often unconscious, experiences of the subjects. Try asking a top sales person why they are so good. They don't know, they just are. Their techniques, patterns, beliefs, skills and values are all things that they live and do instinctively.

NEURO – An understanding of the brain and its functions. The nervous system through which experience is received and processed through the five senses.

LINGUISTIC – Verbal and non-verbal communication to ourselves and others. Language and non verbal communication systems through which neural representations are coded, ordered, and given meaning.

PROGRAMMING – Behaviour and thinking patterns. The ability to organise our communication and neurological systems to achieve specific desired goals and results.

NLP is the study of the structure of subjective experience. As such, it is not about theories, which are the basis of most other psychologies and science generally. Looking at human nature from this different standpoint was the key ingredient to what has led to such a treasure chest of discoveries.

On the lighter side of definitions, John Grinder once said, on a presentation I attended, that with coming up with the term NLP it was obvious that Richard and himself knew very little about marketing! Richard Bandler developed his reputation by transforming the lives of people that the 'experts' had either given up on or were under long term care.

That as may be but in my experience of life, commercial and otherwise, the two of them have contributed more to the field of human communication that the rest added together. Ask many professionals to cure a simple phobia of heights, public speaking, cold calling for example and see what they can actually do for you. Ask any NLP Practitioner and it will be gone five minutes later. NLP only measures success by results. It moved the field of psychology from the academic to the practical. Be warned, many in the community are moving it back to the academic and intellectual.

Bandler and Grinder developed a unique system of asking questions to gather precise information. The more they studied top performers, the more they noticed about how we communicate and the more they noticed the differences between the average and the outstanding.

They successfully transferred these communication patterns to others (without extensive training) and they too produced outstanding results. Clearly an unprecedented quantum leap had been made in accelerating the learning process. From the early work, research and development has been continued. Documentation on the successes of the application of NLP is hard to believe, though there is now substantial evidence. For years now, Dr Bandler has studied how geniuses used their minds to accomplish what they did and has repeatedly replicated the results that they achieved – so successfully that NLP is now a well-established international phenomenon.

NLP Modelling is the process of replicating particular behaviours. To model effectively, certain skills are required which include sensory awareness, verbal and non-verbal skills to elicit quality information. There are three key areas of behaviour to model: belief systems, strategies and physiology. The test for the model is in producing the same, or similar results in someone else. An important distinction is to be made between theories and models. A theory is more concerned with answering 'Why' questions. A model is concerned with answering 'How?' Modelling is the process that requires knowing what to do to answer 'How?'

The first step of NLP modelling is to find a skill that you would like to have. The second stage is to find somebody who excels at that skill. Then the NLP Practitioner studies that person until they have established how exactly they do that. This is then tested on others until the patterns that make the difference have been clearly identified. This modelling process is quite complex and developing in sophistication all the time. There are now other disciplines and research being carried out taking these ideas further. It is not however necessary to understand or even appreciate the modelling process to benefit from NLP. In fact, all that is necessary is to adopt the patterns of behaviour of outstanding performers found from somebody else's modelling of them. Rapport and motivation skills, for example, have been studied so much by NLP experts that there is a great wealth of knowledge available. This book is not about the modelling process itself; it is the result of behavioural modelling of sales superstars (please be aware that most courses on NLP will be about learning the trail of techniques that have been left by NLP modellers, not the modelling process itself).

It has long been known that we communicate in three ways: through the words we use, tonality and body language. What is less widely known is the influence of each category. One often quoted major study concluded that they are Words 7%, Tonality 38% and Body Language 55% (Please note that to draw accurate conclusions from any study, the parameters and objectives of what was being measured have to be looked at. Secondly, this short conclusion ignores the substantial overlap between the three; they are clearly not separate. Even so, the implications for business communication are far reaching). In business, if your staff are trained only in what to say they are missing out on 93% of their potential! NLP teaches how to develop rapport in seconds by using all your communication channels. In the area of words, sales scripts, questions, closing techniques and above all listening skills have been revolutionised. The advanced language patterns of NLP can teach excellence in communication skills. NLP then, is the art and science of achievement.

NLP is the study of the difference between competence and excellence, in terms of practical skills that can be passed on to others. It is therefore a learning model. In addition to modelling and the resultant methodology, there are also the NLP presuppositions. These are the model of the attitudes and beliefs that have been found to be true for the top communicators and in people who are very successful at what they do.

F – Other benefits of sales skills to entrepreneurs

Entrepreneurs find themselves often in selling situations, for which all the content of this book is valuable. For example, when you are selling your ideas to the bank for an unsecured loan, you will have to have a written plan. Get a couple of friends that are in business to go through it and ask those difficult questions before the bank manager does. Write a draft 2 and a draft 3 and, after every live presentation, improve it from what was said at the meeting, use your friends as free consultants. At the end of the day though, a bank, whatever they say, will be most interested in the security for the loan.

If you are presenting to venture capitalists, their main interest will be in their assessment of management's ability to put the plan into action, and not the cleverness of the business idea. Always check for current government or other schemes on offer. If you are literally starting out, it may be a good idea to offer something really special, if not free to your first customer. That way you get a client to refer to and build upon.

Another valuable area for applying selling skills is getting customers to pay up. The best way to achieve this is to sell before you buy. I launched my audio CD business this way by getting customers and then going into production. It is a much better route than raising finance. Using sales income as your venture capitalist is my philosophy. Traditional business has so many overheads with it, too many of them fixed. In this Internet world you can avoid most if not all of these and launch and develop a business so much more cheaply and less riskily.

There are three types of purchases – those that you pay for before you consume (aeroplane flight, theatre ticket, office rent), those while or immediately after you consume (restaurant, shopping), and those that where you send an invoice out (telephone, consultancy). Always try to move your business to the former and your suppliers to the latter. When you have invoices outstanding, persuading somebody to send a cheque is a sales process, where all the techniques in this book can be applied. The sales process is finished on the day the cheque clears.

There is a world of difference between an entrepreneur and employee mind set. Many employees are put off by the stresses that entrepreneurs have to bear. Little do they appreciate that most entrepreneurs in their moment of maximum stress would not swap their lot to be an employee again and have those stresses. Referring to the saying, 'having all your eggs in one basket', it has always baffled me why banks and lending institutions consider somebody with one job a good risk to lend money to. Personally I would not lend a sizeable amount of money to someone with one insecure source of income. Taking higher mortgages than they can really afford, they can find themselves being owned and dictated to by the house they live in, whilst under the illusion that they own it. Maintaining their quality of life through credit cards then erodes their long term prosperity. You cannot run a successful business like this. In your selling, think long term.

These high short-term costs are a significant barrier to entrepreneurship, which is about investing now for the long term. Mortgages, credit cards and loans, used for have-now-pay-later instant gratification, are the enemies of entrepreneurial success. You have to think long-term investment, short-term sacrifice. Employees are paid as they go along.

Entrepreneurs work now with the intention of gaining a return from that month's work for the rest of their lives, and then to leave an inheritance. Building a business with all of this overhead is like trying to take off from an aircraft carrier with a plane full of lead. You need to keep light of any unnecessary burdens. If applicable, your spouse has to not only be supportive of you but living light as well. It is pointless in building a business to make these early and crucial sales and not have that money reinvested in the enterprise.

Employees do what the boss tells them and are motivated by being told what to do by a superior. This is done positively through raises, promotions and, negatively, the threat of redundancy and rebukes. Entrepreneurs are largely motivated by themselves. They actually have more bosses than the employee – customers, bank manager, staff demanding salaries, suppliers, and usually the spouse as well puts the pressure on. Breaking away from an employee mindset is I think the greatest challenge to an entrepreneur. Becoming self-employed is a part move in this direction, but is not fully there.

The two most vital resources you have are your time and money. So my philosophy on selling is simple:

'If it costs money, there is a better way. Look and you shall find.'
'If it costs time, there is a better way. Look and you shall find.'

If you can present to an audience of 20 people, you are probably going to be more sales effective than presenting one to one. Quite often, travel to see clients is very draining on time. Can technology help perhaps, video conferencing, presentation on the web page? You need to be always asking yourself, 'How, like a modern computer, do you achieve two or more things at the same time?'

I consider there are five types of entrepreneur, as I first discussed in my book *'Be Your Best and Beyond ... Entrepreneur'*:

- **Lifestyle Entrepreneurs** – working their hobby
- **Profit Entrepreneurs** – purely in business for the money
- **Formula Entrepreneurs** – franchisees and network marketers
- **Empire Entrepreneurs** – wanting to build a major corporation
- **Creative Entrepreneurs** – inventors, artists, authors.

You may be a mix of more than one depending on your motivations. All of these have to sell. Some, such as franchisees, will have a system and a manual for how to find and deal with customers. Network marketers, who build a network of customers who in turn are agents, are not really selling at all in the strictest sense. However, they largely work alone although with upline support. The chapter on self-motivation will be of particular interest to them. Lifestyle entrepreneurs have the advantage that they have a strong passion and enthusiasm for what they are selling. Their weakness is that they often sell the wrong thing and pay little heed to the customer, being focused on what they love. Whichever type you are, this book is aimed at your needs.

Progress now:

What type of Entrepreneur am I/do I want to be?

Summary of key points in chapter

➤ My target in writing this book is to give entrepreneurs and other non-sales professionals selling skills quickly.

➤ If you look at the various skills of sales you will soon realise that you not only have done it before, but you have done it before very well and many times.

➤ The advantage in being a beginner is that learning can progress far quicker with this book.

➤ Once you decide to focus on listening, business will increasingly come your way.

➤ Selling is first and foremost about having a pride, a passion and belief in what you are offering.

➢ This book assumes no previous knowledge of selling and goes straight to the techniques that top sales professionals use.

➢ Since it's creation NLP (Neuro-Linguistic Programming) has continually grown in interest around the world.

➢ NLP is essentially a model of excellence and achievement of 'what works best'.

➢ NLP, the now established psychology of achievement has contributed a great deal to this work.

➢ Marketing should always come before selling activity.

➢ People are happy to be influenced if it improves their situation.

➢ We all perceive a situation differently.

➢ This book is comprehensive and covers everything you need to know about selling.

➢ There is a world of difference between an entrepreneur and employee mind set.

➢ There are five classifications of business entrepreneur:
  • Lifestyle Entrepreneurs working their hobby
  • Profit Entrepreneurs purely in business for the money
  • Formula Entrepreneurs franchisees and network marketers
  • Empire Entrepreneurs wanting to build a major corporation
  • Creative Entrepreneurs inventors, artists, authors

2

Sales – The Big Picture

'A drop of honey catches more flies than a gallon of gall.'
Abraham Lincoln

'If you can dream it, then you can achieve it.
You will get all you want in life if you help enough other people
get what they want.'
Zig Ziglar

This chapter ...

A	Why do people buy things
B	The features of what you have to sell
C	Benefits of features
D	Listening to needs
E	Matching the benefits of your features to their needs
F	The main benefit you offer
G	Time Leveraged Selling (TLS)

A – Why do people buy things

Progress now:

Think now of five things that you have ever bought, such as a newspaper, car, house, holiday, chocolate, shampoo, stationery, a computer, pint of beer, new suit ...

a.

b.

c.

d.

e.

Now, for one of the above, make a list of the reasons that you bought this item. What or who influenced you? How much importance did you put on the price? Did the packaging influence you? Did the person selling it to you convince you? Was how you felt at the time a deciding factor? What did you believe the product or service would do for you? Is this a product you have always bought and you rigidly stick to this brand? What were your criteria for making a decision? If there was a sales person involved what about them did you like and what did you not like?

a.

b.

c.

d.

e.

Now considering the other items, were the factors similar or different? What can you conclude from this? Turning it around, what have you learnt about what you must do to sell your proposal to others effectively?

The first rule of effective selling is to put yourself in the buyer's shoes. In other words, see the communication from the point of view of the recipient.

People buy things for a variety of reasons. They must have a need or a perceived need with the cash or credit to back it up. Their strongest and most urgent needs will get priority.

So, with this knowledge your first task is to target the segment of the market, at the time that you think would be most appropriate for your proposal. If you are selling meat pies don't ring vegetarians! Or to put it another way: a mousetrap, however advanced, only works if there are mice about. Finding where the mice are in business is called marketing. Enticing them to the mousetrap is called sales. Of course the difference being is that our mousetrap is full of quality cheese without any trap! Marketing is a specialist area in itself. Although I give tips in this work, it is predominantly about selling for entrepreneurs. Who needs what I have to offer? Who could need it? Who, why, what, when and where are the opportunities? There are some good reference books in the bibliography on marketing.

B – The features of what you have to sell

The first piece of the sales process is to understand all the features, the attributes of your product(s) or service(s). Here are three different examples:

a. A Karate Club
The club teaches the Wado Ryu style of Karate and runs adult sessions on Tuesday, Thursday and Saturday at various locations. It also offers a choice of times and venues for children's classes. It cost £6 per session for an adult, which will comprise a thorough workout, covering all areas of fitness including stretching, muscle tone etc. The Karate spirit along with meditation and mind discipline skills will be taught. There are ten grades/belts to black belt level. Every March there is a Kumite (Tournament) held in Horsham, Sussex. It is open to both genders and all ages, and there are several senior black belt instructors. All details can be found on:
www.horshamkarateclub.com

b. Curriculum Vitae Writing Service
Our service will design your CV using an expert in sales and marketing. The CV will be less than three sides long of A4 and it will be thoroughly proof read. The price is £99.99

c. Specialty Pens

Our pens are five inches long with a thick, easy rubber grip. They come in four different colours – red, blue, brown and black. A company or personal identification can be printed on them. The cost is £1 each.

Progress now:

For whatever product and service you offer, write down the *features*.

Okay, you are at the *first step* of the sales process, this is just the start. Most people in selling make the mistake of just selling the features. It is a good start but a sad mistake. If they went to the next stage, their sales results would be greatly increased.

C – Benefits of features

A feature in itself is a factual statement of truth, no more than a description. When you start to look at what benefits can come from those features, you are starting to really sell. To find the benefit of any particular feature, all you have to do is ask some very basic questions of it. *'What is the benefit to someone of this feature?'* This will leave you with a list of features followed by a statement, bridged by *which means that*.

Using our examples:

a) Karate classes for adults are on Tuesdays, Thursday and Saturdays
   - *which means that* you have a good choice of when it fits into your timetable
   - *which means that* you can attend all of them and accelerate your progression
   - *which means that* if you get behind for whatever reason you can catch up.

b) Your CV will be designed by an expert in sales and marketing
   - *which means that* techniques of persuasion are fully used in the content
   - *which means that* you can spend your time looking for job opportunities.

c) Our pens are five inches long with a thick easy rubber grip
   - *which means that* they will fit into your pocket easily
   - *which means that* they don't slip when you are writing with them.

Of course, for each feature there could be several benefits.

Progress now:

Write down at least ten features of what you are selling, together with two benefits for each feature:

1.

2.

3.

4.

5.

6.

7.

8.

9.

10.

You now have twenty reasons why somebody should buy from you!

Okay, you are at the *second step* of four of the sales process. Most people in selling who understand and know all the features don't appreciate the benefits of what they have to offer. If you don't know all the benefits of what you have to offer, you can be sure your prospective customer won't. So, if you understand both features and benefits, well done, your sales results will significantly increase when you apply what you have done so far.

It is a very good start, but sadly lacking a key element. If you progress to the next stage, your sales results will be greatly increased.

D – Listening to needs

So far, we have concentrated on knowing about what you have to offer. Let us change tack completely for a moment and put our attention totally on a prospective customer. If someone is considering joining a Karate School or having a CV professionally designed, what needs are they trying to satisfy?

a) **Karate school** – fitness, self defence, getting out and meeting people, networking, mental discipline ...

b) **CV service** – a new job, which breaks down to interviews, a livelihood ...

c) **A pen** – writing, must not leak in a pocket, clips to side of jacket ...

All individuals are different and their needs or perceived needs are what motivates them to make the initial enquiry or respond favourably to someone approaching them. These needs could include a whole range of things. Their needs can be emotional as well as tangible. Help others get what they want.

Want	Need
Washing Powder	Clean Clothes
Rental Car	Transportation
Food	Hunger

The want is just the answer to the need that they have come to. There may be other ways of satisfying that need. There may be other products and services that are also useful. A need is thus always an opportunity. He who can best satisfy it will win the business.

Progress now:

> From the two last people you sold something to, what motivated them to buy from you? What basic needs were being satisfied?

Okay, you are at the *third step* of the sales process. You now understand features, benefits and needs. Well done. Your sales results will greatly increase by applying these simple yet effective principles. However, you still have not reached your potential. There is one more step you can take that can make an equal leap in your results.

E – Matching the benefits of your features to their needs

You know your features and the benefits that they offer. You have listened to your prospective customers and established what their needs are. You now need to marry the two together. First list their needs in priority order. Don't try to be clever on this but work with them. For each need in order, list what benefit your product or service offers that satisfies that particular need. When you have tied these up, most people will buy from you, because they can see that their criteria are being met.

So the basic sales process is:

1. Know all the features of what you offer.
2. Know and write down all the benefits of those features.
3. Listen to each potential customer until you know their needs.
4. Tell them the benefits you offer that satisfy their needs.

Simple isn't it? Well this is how top performing sales professionals do it. It is simple and works if you apply it. Of course you may find that when you know their needs, your offer might not satisfy them. You have two choices. To change what you offer, particularly if you keep getting this feedback. Good business at the end of the day is supplying people with what they need, or think they need, and have money to back it.

Keep asking yourself questions like:

- Where is my market moving?
- Am I evolving with it?
- What am I selling?
- In what way is it unique?

If you find selling hard work, then you might be offering the wrong thing. Ask people what they want, listen to them and then offer it to them. Don't assume you know what they want or will buy. They will think differently from you, having a whole different set of logic. To help find opportunities, you need to be focused and looking all the time, covered at length in my book, *'Entrepreneur'*. Here, of course, we are moving out of the area of sales and into marketing.

The other area of sales that we have not touched on yet is how to find prospective customers in the first place, to make our pitch to. Again, this is largely the realm of marketing, advertising, mail shots, web sites, telesales and networking.

The best way to sell is to find something where you are swimming with the tide and where the tide is not likely to change directions in the near future. When the tide changes, change with it. If you find yourself in a market of over-supply, then you need to differentiate your product more. I have found though, that business people in all industries when asked; 'What are the thirty benefits to a customer buying your product?' could not give me an answer. The world of selling is full of enormous opportunity!

Techniques can be learnt from reading this book and can be applied to effect the same day. The beauty of being an entrepreneur is that you have the ability to improve your income. Many people have to wait for an annual review!

F – The main benefit you offer

There is an old saying amongst sales professionals. *'People buy people first and whatever else second.'* It means that part of what a customer buys is the privilege of dealing with you. We all like to deal with people we like, trust and have faith in. Some people, on learning selling, believe that they have to change their personality to become a good sales person. Not at all. I have personally met a whole range of top sales superstars of wildly different personalities. There is a general image of such a person, but it is often not true. I know many such people who are quite shy and introverted, which is the exact opposite of what people view them as. Anyone can be a good listener. You see, for selling, the important personality is that of the person you are selling to, not yours. So work with your own personality, do not try and change it, but become a better and more capable you.

Progress now:

What is special about you, from the customer's perspective?

G – Time Leveraged Selling (TLS)

The best types of customers can be summed up as follows:

- those that have a need for what you offer
- those that are financially secure
- those that are growing
- those that are very choosy in who they give their business to (once you get them it is hard for a competitor to take them away)
- those that make repeat orders
- those that give large order customers
- those that help you develop other customers.

Assess the value of each of your customers by giving them a point for each of the above. Ask yourself what you can do to give them a higher grading.

The first way to save time is right at the start by doing some thinking relative to what you offer and figure out the best market opportunities. Those that have a need and the money to pay for it. There can be many ways to market though, depending on what business you are in exactly. Before you start, you need to define a profile or profiles of potential customers, and, if you include companies, who within those companies would make or influence a purchasing decision.

For the entrepreneur, the biggest limit to sales growth is your set-up. If you are self-employed, your income can be totally dependent upon your labour, whether you are a plumber or a motivational trainer. This is not good business long-term. The best way to make money is passively, i.e. it comes in without your having to be there. You also have very limited growth potential if increases in sales can only be met by you. Also, as a one person band, in practice you will find that the time you spend on sales activity robs your billing time. The formula is just not an efficient one for making money. Whilst the enterprise is dependent on you, the more vulnerable you are.

Be wary of selling what you want to do, instead of listening for needs and then providing accordingly. Most entrepreneurs limit their business potential by focusing on their 'dream and passion'. That is fine but it makes sense to get the business financially secure first. You get what you focus on. If your overwhelming focus is to make money, then automatically your mind will be geared to seeing opportunities to doing just that. Job satisfaction will be a more secondary motivation. I cannot stress it enough – business is about providing for somebody else what *they* want. Selling is far more about listening than talking.

Entrepreneurs often have more shortage of cash and time than other people in business. So you have to be brighter and more creative. There is an abundance of ways – whatever you do – to advertise in a way that costs you no up-front cash or time. This book advertises my services as an author, speaker, motivator, consultant, coach and trainer – all of which I am and offer. Well, it has now! It is currently costing me no time or money. It certainly took time to write but I am being paid for that in terms of royalties. I have also set up a career coaching business. It cost me nothing to set up. That is right – absolutely nothing. I approached recruitment websites such as **CVPoster.com** and offered them a sales commission to put all of my services on their site. Interestingly they did not have to pay anything to set up an extra income stream either. Their clients now get added services from them and everyone is a winner.

Find out who could be a reseller of your product or service for a commission. That way you do not have to provide cash or time. If you are the recipient of a telesales call or a mail-shot letter, turn it around. You have just been presented with the contact details of a prospect. The call, after all, is on their bill!

Email

A lot of communication these days is through e-mail. There are a few golden rules to make it happen.

- Firstly, make sure the subject line grabs attention and will ensure that the e-mail is opened because it is meaningful and personal. Everyone receives so much junk mail, we have all developed a trigger happy delete finger. If you have had a recent chat with someone, put 'Recent Chat' for example.

- The second rule is keep it short, simple and to the point. If it is to confirm something the subject line alone can suffice.
- Thirdly, develop some standard letter responses that you can just paste in with a click.
- Fourthly, have at least one default signature which carries information on you and what you are selling, web page, any offers etc.

Progress now:

What action can you take now to leverage your selling time?

H – Big picture tips

Is what you offer special or are you indistinguishable from your competitors. If you are not special, you need to do something to make it so. In the book which I co-authored with Kevin Uphill on how to buy and sell a business for capital wealth, we cover in depth how to make your business stand out. Before you start selling, make sure that something special is included.

If you talk or write excitedly and enthusiastically, you can virtually let the words take care of themselves. First get their attention, then interest, followed by building desire and tell them what action they have to take. The common sales acronym A I D A (Attention, Interest, Desire, Action) is a good basic reminder to live by. One of the biggest drawbacks that professional sales people have is that they come over as just that. This does not get attention and interest and usually triggers off a, 'defence against sales pitches' type of response.

Remember that other people saying you are good is 100 times better than your saying it yourself. What are you most likely be influenced by? A friend saying that her local Indian restaurant is the best in the world – she thoroughly recommends it – or an advert in the local paper saying they are the best in the world.

Get the telephone bill up and get out and meet people. You won't make any useful contacts sat at home. If you have something that might genuinely help me in my life then contact me (via web page at **www.alexmcmillan.com**). There – a free lead for you for reading my book. I am always open to ideas.

If you are doing some canvassing calls, make sure you finish on a positive conversation. In fact, set your goals not by number of calls or time spent but by achievements. Decide on three positive sales calls per day. That way, if it takes five minutes or five hours, three calls or thirty is irrelevant. If you do just a little and are rejected, there is a stronger tendency to remember the experience as rejection. Focus only on the achievements, the rest is irrelevant.

There are some different rules for selling to corporates or to individuals. Individuals make their own decisions with money coming from their pocket. Corporates can have much deeper pockets and the decision maker is not spending his personal money. They can also have a long and complicated decision-making process. Always test if you are making prospecting calls by trying ten with one approach and ten with another to see what works best.

If someone does not buy now, do two things. One, diary them for a call at a future date and then ask them for a referral of someone they know that might be interested now. Always remember that people are obsessive about spending money – it is our favourite thing to do. Just imagine how much money is changing hands every second through cash, cheques, credit cards and so on – it is a colossal flow. There are more £10 notes changing hands every second than drops of water flowing over Niagara Falls, and this book is full of buckets! All you have to do is get on the receiving end of that flow and get your share.

Remember that at first you need to arouse their curiosity, not satisfy it. Always ask what else to existing clients, focus on their end results. Make it easy for them to get onto the customer train, perhaps by a small start and then upgrade. If practical, let the prospective customers experience as fully as possible your product or service. Let them get used to the idea of being a customer.

The Internet now lets you sell worldwide from your bedroom. Personally though I am not a big believer in having your own web page. Mainly because everybody and their friend has one and the time and costs in operating them and marketing them can be excessive. What I am a big believer in is using other people's web pages free of charge. That way they get the burden of maintaining the site, marketing it and all the costs. You can have the advantage of being on many such web sites. All you have to do is find complimentary sites and offer them a commission on anything of yours that they sell.

You can also write articles for free all over the Internet. Whatever the subject, there is a demand. If you sell cuddly toys, write an article on the role of cuddly toys in early learning and surf the net for relevant sites. All you need is your name and email address at the end. I have picked up some of my best clients this way.

I asked a self-made millionaire once, how easy is it to make a million. He said, 'it is simple – any fool can do it. It baffles me why more don't.' You know what, the rest of my research agrees with him. What often stops people is that they are making it too complicated.

Progress now:

Have a stroke of genius right now!

3

Plotting the Path to Success

'Per Ardua Ad Astra'
'Through Struggle to the Stars' – motto of the Royal Air Force

'Efforts and courage are not enough without purpose
and direction.'

John F Kennedy

'If you shoot for the stars and hit the moon, it's OK, but you have got
to shoot for something. A lot of people don't even shoot.'

Confucius

This chapter ...

A   The importance of clarifying sales objectives
B   My sales objectives
C   The action plan
D   Reacting to feedback
E   The power of multiple perspectives
F   Future customer analysis
G   What business are you in?

A – The importance of clarifying sales objectives

Establishing clear objectives is one of the key things that identifies highly successful entrepreneurs. It brings with it commitment, direction and motivation. The more committed you are to something, the easier it seems to become.

Have you watched friends start up their own business from home, as a fly on the wall? To me they fit into two groups. Those who are permanently on the phone, busy writing and so on, with a real sense of urgency. At the end of the day they cannot believe that it went so quickly, there is so much more they wanted to achieve. If you ask them for five minutes of their time, they say no. Then there are those who seem to be constantly searching through directories and old files or surfing the Internet. If you ask them if they can spare five minutes the answer is, yeah sure. The difference is usually that the former group are working towards clear objectives and are not prepared to digress away from their focus. If that means doing something they don't like, they have the attitude, 'I'm going to get through it as quickly as possible in order to get to my objectives beyond.' Their passion for what they are doing, married with a clear focus, generates all the motivation, energy and confidence they need. They know exactly what they want to achieve and have a plan for getting it.

The second group will always work on what they enjoy most, or hate least, then justify to themselves and others why they are working in the way that they do, often getting very defensive. Ring any bells?

As an entrepreneur, you will find yourself doing more than one person's job and you have to budget your time accordingly. It is easy to fall into the trap of focusing on what you enjoy or what pushes you the most. You need to make at least part of your passion running the business itself. As such, you will apportion your time according to what is in the business's best interest. When you go out to see a prospective client to sell, look forward to it, get excited. Somebody is affording you their time to listen to your ideas and proposals. Think of the business as a separate entity to you and ask what its needs are. If you need to budget two days a week, or one hour per day to selling then, do so and keep to it.

You should have an overall business plan of some description. I want you in a moment to write down your sales plan, objectives and a timescale for when you want to achieve them. Be realistic rather than optimistic. The trick of success is to set goals that you are fairly confident of hitting and then raise them slightly. Have the big plan and break it down into small manageable chunks, representing staging points to success. In sales, we say, 'by the yard is hard but by the inch is a cinch'. By focusing on small steps at a time, your confidence is never threatened and your motivation is high as you are always near to the next step.

B – My sales objectives

Write down in specific terms what you want to achieve. Keep everything in the positive. Think in terms of what you want, not what you don't want.

1. **Determine an exact sales figure**. Break this down to a weekly if not daily achievement target. Include non financial sales targets such as number of phone calls, visits, contacts, tasks.
2. **Test each goal** by asking questions of it, 'Are you prepared to do whatever it takes to achieve this?' 'Is this the best goal I can set myself?'
3. **Establish what exactly you will have to do** to achieve your sales targets.
4. **Type out the plan**, broken down into objectives for each quarter, then month, then week and perhaps by day depending on the nature of your business. Think of each quarter's objectives as rungs on a ladder. Then stick it on the wall or somewhere prominent where you will see it every day. Goals in drawers or in a file in your laptop are no use, you need to keep reminding yourself so as to stay on focus.

Let us make a start at number 1: What is it that you want to achieve?

If you have just started out, the first thing to do in selling is to network amongst your current contacts. It makes no sense to prospect from cold contacts (mails shot, advertising, telesales), if you have warm contacts. Write a list of everyone you know. Initially do not concern yourself if they are useful or not, just think of as many names as you can.

Progress now:

My Overall Sales Plan:

From now on, forget past results. Decide, in detail, what you want to achieve. Okay, so we are going to define precisely what we want and then develop a clear plan to get it. List everything you want, take as much time as you need. A new house, a sports car, lots of money, two luxury holidays per year, a management buy-out, to sell most in your company, write a book, lose that extra stone of weight ... Be as detailed as you can, for example, what new house exactly, what car exactly, how much money? Do this now on the following page in pencil and change it until you are totally satisfied. When you have done that, imagine you are in the future at the time that you have all those things. Looking back to now, see what it was that you had to do that led to those achievements. This will help you in developing a clear plan and knowing exactly what you have to do and also what you don't have to do. If you are doing something that is not supporting you towards your objectives, drop or change it. Looking back from a future point is important as, firstly, it is a final check that you are totally sure that it is what you want to achieve. Secondly, by putting your achievements in the past tense, your brain codes them as reality, as opposed to possible future events.

Progress now:

What I want:

1.

2.

3.

4.

5.

6.

7.

8.

9.

10.

11.

12.

13.

14.

15.

Now, divide your list in terms of what you want to achieve within 12 months (ring the number) and those over a longer period. When you have done that put both lists in order of priority.

C – The action plan

How I am going to get what I want:

1.

2.

3.

4.

5.

6.

7.

8.

9.

10.

11.

12.

13.

14.

15.

The above is what I am going to achieve by _____

Signed _____ Dated _____

Witnessed _____ Dated _____

Make a copy of the previous two pages and stick them on the wall where you work. This will constantly remind you of what you are working towards and provide a challenge every time you do something which is not taking you towards your goals.

Effective selling is relationship building through the art of dovetailing your objectives to those of your future customer. To do this, you need to establish both your own and your target's objectives. Having established your own objectives, you help your customer to ascertain what his objectives really are; then you show him how to achieve them, in a way that is consistent with the realisation of your own objectives.

The sales process is in fact an objective-setting exercise:

- setting objectives for yourself
- eliciting your future customer's objectives
- dovetailing the two together.

Now that you have a clearly laid-out plan, the next essential stage is to get going!

D – Reacting to feedback

Once you have realised how vital it is to listen and observe for feedback, you now have to use that knowledge skilfully. You must be flexible to continually alter your response to reflect a developing and changing situation. As you gather input through a presentation, you must change your approach to match the new situation. Knowledge is only power when it is acted upon. Or to put it another way:

**'If you keep doing the same things,
you will keep getting the same results.'**

'You trim your sails to the wind that blows.'

First read the signs (observation and calibration) and then adjust your behaviour accordingly to home in on your target.

What exactly is it that makes flexible behaviour so hard? Perhaps it is the fear of failure, or that you are not confident that your calibrations and deductions of what your future customer is thinking are right. In this case, what you are doing is not producing the results – so try something else.

If sales presentations were suits, some would perfectly fit the customer and some would not. You may have won some accounts and lost others without really knowing the reason for either. My aim in this chapter has been to show you the importance of flexibility, to put those lost sales into the winning camp. When analysing sales success, most people concentrate on what they did and then what the potential client did as if they were two separate entities. I would like you to start thinking of successful sales presentations as when two people behave as one.

This approach is in direct contrast to the 'numbers game' mentality. While credible evidence can be produced to show that selling *is* a numbers game, it is a dangerous belief to adopt. It firstly puts you in the frame of mind to accept the situations where you lost. 'Well, you can't win them all' say the supporters of this belief. 'Why not?' is what I want to ask. After each situation where you did not get all that you wanted, ask yourself two questions.

- 'What could I have done differently to get a better result?'
- 'What can I do, right now, to change the result?'

These questions will focus your mind on learning from your experience and concentrating on further action.

E – The power of multiple perspectives

As already discussed, our personal perceptions filter memories of events by generalising, making distortions and deletions. We cannot not do this. Therefore you will find that if you get two people to meet and then ask them independently to write a one-page summary on what transpired, you will have a surprise. Reading such reports, it is hard to believe that the participants ever met. This phenomenon is the reason why many sales are lost – remember the sales representative who thought things were going his way and was surprised when no order appeared?

Our perceptions of the world are completely individual to us, and as such have large holes. The technique of 'viewing positions' allows us to get outside of our own models of what transpired and see it as if we were somebody else.

Imagine that you could take the two people in business you most admire with you on every visit to give you feedback afterwards. This information would considerably accelerate your learning from each experience, wouldn't it? After all, making mistakes, as long as we recognise them, is how we learn. And learning is how we progress to excellence and peak performance.

A 'viewing position' is the point of view from which we see the 'world' at any particular time. Developing the skill of taking regular differing viewing positions is simple and requires no more than a vivid imagination.

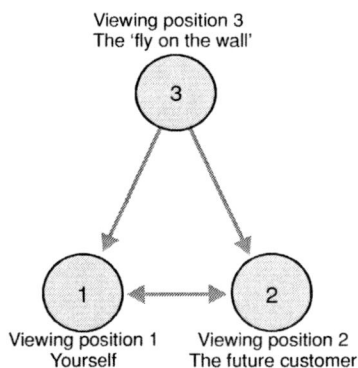

Viewing position 3
The 'fly on the wall'

There are three main viewing positions:

- First position: the sales representative.
- Second position: the future customer.
- Third position: a fly on the wall, noticing the communication between you simultaneously.

Viewing position 1
Yourself

Viewing position 2
The future customer

Following each presentation, take fifteen minutes with a pen and paper in a place where you will not be disturbed. First, run through the presentation again in your mind from start to finish. Run it slowly, and listen and watch as much as possible. With the knowledge of how the meeting actually progressed it will probably make more sense to you than it did at the time.

- From the first position (your own), write down any notes that come to mind. Ask yourself what would you do differently if you could wind the clock back.
- Now take the second position, this time imagining that you were the customer, looking through his eyes. What do you see? What do you now feel about the presentation of the person who has come into your office? You will find that doing this exercise helps you tremendously in realising why the customer reacted the way he did. Write some more notes. What would you now do differently with the totally new perspective of the customer's viewpoint?
- Now, take the third position. In your mind, imagine that you are in a cinema watching a film of the presentation taken by a hidden camera. Imagine you have a remote control and you can freeze-frame, go slower, or replay selected sequences. What do you notice from this position? In all three positions, you will find it works better if you can allocate different locations (try standing or sitting in three different places in the

room, as suggested in the previous diagram). This will also help to identify which role you are playing if you run it through more than once or do it in a group.

Although it may seem a bit strange at first, in fifteen minutes or so, this simple exercise will provide you with six months' worth of work experience – an accelerated learning path, I'm sure you will agree. Psychologically what is happening is broadly as follows. Our unconscious mind records all that we are seeing, feeling and hearing. However so that our conscious mind is not overloaded, it filters out most of the incoming data, concentrating on what seems the most important at the time. Consciously, therefore, we don't usually have access to all that we know. When you use your imagination you access the unconscious and all the information that is there. What we are doing in this exercise is calling up the relevant files, viewing them at our leisure and then consciously drawing deductions and conclusions from them.

This exercise will take you from being clever to being wise. Its purpose is to provide you with the maximum amount of feedback possible. With that feedback, you must be flexible to change your style accordingly in order to control the outcome of subsequent meetings.

F – Future customer analysis

Each prospective customer needs to be analysed. Knowledge is potential power and certainly helps when you call them again. Throughout the book, we will be looking at ways to get even more value from this knowledge.

Name: Position:

Company:

Address:

Telephone:

E-Mail

Web Page:

Words: Repeated words

Repeated phrases

Favourite metaphor

Tonality:	Volume:	Quiet / Loud
	Pitch:	Low / High
	Tone :	Soft / Harsh
	Speed:	Slow / Fast
	Spaces:	Short / Long

Language:

Pictures	*Feelings*	*Logic*	*Sounds*	*Smell/Taste*
See	Touch	Think	Heard	Smelt
Show	Warm	Know	Said	Taste
Focus	Pressure	Change	Listen	Sweet
_____	_____	_____	_____	_____
_____	_____	_____	_____	_____
_____	_____	_____	_____	_____
_____	_____	_____	_____	_____
_____	_____	_____	_____	_____

Decision-Making Style: Moving towards / Moving away

Positive / Negative

Self / Written / Others

Similarities / Differences

Generalisations / Specifics

Past / Present / Future

Short-term / Long-term

Task / Relationships

Money

Numbers

Places

People

Result of Call:

Next Contact/Objective:

G – What business are you in?

Progress now:

What business are you in?

As an entrepreneur, you will typically have limited resources and as such you have to become creative and get as much out of any resources as you can. The rule is always to ask a customer if he or she knows of anybody else who may have an interest in the proposal. For that matter, don't just ask customers, ask everyone you talk to. I have won clients from talking to the person next to me in a bus queue. There are even networking groups set up with the sole aim of meeting others. This might be useful, but personally I prefer to go to gatherings which are likely to have people that I have an interest in meeting. When I was in Accountancy Recruitment, I went to financial seminars. Just ask yourself what the most useful types of contacts that you need to make are. Then ask where do they go?

Every adult realistically knows at least another 100 adults. Write down now a list of everyone you know:

- colleagues
- ex-colleagues
- sports club friends
- neighbours
- association memberships
- relatives
- general friends.

Do this until you have at least 100. Now ring them and tell them what you are doing. Every hundred people knows another hundred. So what does that make your potential contact/referral pool. 100 x 100 = 10,000. Wrong – because you forgot the fact that those 10,000 also know at least a 100 people and so on.

Now the real world of people does not always follow the rules of mathematics. They are not all going to ring all the people they know, just for you. But they might bear you in mind when those 100 happen to ring them and what you offer becomes relevant to the conversation. You have a 100 unpaid sales representatives working for you. On top of that, you have no direct cost for advertising.

In fact, the world has many companies with millions and billions of pounds turnover where their entire sales were and are made up from networking (I am currently researching and recruiting successful network marketing and franchising companies for a forthcoming book).

Do you ever get telephoned or mailshotted by companies? Well I do and am grateful for it, unlike everyone else. I immediately tell them about what

I can do for them. 'I can improve the success rate of your letter by at least 25%, would you like to hear how?'

There are people and companies everywhere with hideously abundant needs not being satisfied. Bubbles burst and new ones are formed. Tides subside and rise again. Winds blow with all their might and then settle to a calm. Rivers flood and then there is drought.

A good yachtsman knows how to manipulate nature's forces whatever they are. He will have ideal conditions, but actually his skill is in making the best of what is presented. People looking for sales on the other hand seem to do a lot of hanging about and chatting whilst waiting for ideal conditions to come. You can sail a yacht quite easily to America without a single ideal day on the journey. If you waited for an ideal day for such an objective, you might remain a long time at your port of embarkation!

Glider pilots don't even have an engine to keep them in the sky, and gravity is working on them relentlessly. Yet the skilled glider pilot can fly great distances cross-country. They are motivated and enjoy the challenge of beating the elements by moving from thermal to thermal whilst moving towards their destination. They look ahead to set themselves up. A factory in the distance might generate heat and heat rises. Some days they have good thermals and some bad. Yet even on bad days, there are often thermals that go unspotted. In selling, you might be going through bad market conditions, but there will still be opportunities and you only need one to get working on.

The business you are really in is 'customer acquisition'. I learnt this myself whilst attending a seminar for a company called ACN (American Communications Network) They entirely use independent representatives, only making contact with people they know. They earn in two ways. Firstly they receive customer acquisition bonuses and a commission on their sales. Imagine getting a commission on someone's phone bill every month. They also start by bringing in two other people as representatives and continue to do so. Then those two bring in two more. This clearly becomes 2, 4, 8, 16, 32 and so on. They have a group expanding all by itself and receive a commission on everyone the group brings in. Like many network or co-operative marketing companies, they focus very well on identifying and profiling who would be an ideal person for their service and their business opportunity.

ACN focuses on utilities, telephone, gas, electricity and the Internet. As they don't invest in advertising, telesales and teams of office-based sales representatives and the like, their operating costs are far lower than those that do. It is a very efficient and cheaper way to provide electricity etc to their customers. Imagine being an agent and getting a commission every time a customer you acquired turned on a switch or picked up the phone! Nobody finds gas, phone or electricity supply interesting. They themselves like cheaper bills and they figure they also know some other people who would. The customers and their agents share between them what has been saved on expensive advertising etc. They launched their business in the early 1990s and had a turnover of $2million in 1993, which by the time of writing, has topped $400million with a listing as the 22nd fastest growing company in America! The point is that if you ask one of their directors what business they are in, they will answer customer acquisition. I suggest whatever business you are in, get out of it and get into customer acquisition and only stop when you have $400m worth of them! Without customers there is no business.

4

Empowering Beliefs – the Foundation for Success

'Don't be afraid to take a big step if one is indicated. You can't cross a chasm in two small jumps.'

David Lloyd George

'If people only knew how hard I work to gain my mastery, it wouldn't seem so wonderful at all.'

Michelangelo

This chapter ...

A   What are beliefs?
B   Why are beliefs important?
C   The effect of beliefs on your selling
D   Beliefs of top performers
E   Supporting and limiting beliefs
F   How to make your beliefs supporting
G   A belief-change exercise
H   Your turn to change your beliefs
I   Group belief change

A – What are beliefs?

Here are some different ways I define beliefs. Take a few minutes considering the meaning and significance of each to selling.

- A belief is not about reality, but it is effectively reality for you.
- Beliefs once established become self-fulfilling.
- Belief systems are software for the mind.
- Whether you believe you can or cannot, you are right.
- A belief is a feeling of certainty about something.

A belief is an inner view or conviction, which transcends reason and may not easily be changed by information alone, however contrary to the belief itself. The placebo effect in medicine is due entirely to the creation of a belief, which belies the facts, and has important implications for professional selling.

The thing to realise about beliefs is that your actual behaviour will automatically adapt to meet them. In a conflict between a behaviour and a belief, the latter will usually win. Because of this, beliefs have a powerful self-fulfilling effect. Within the sales context, there are three particularly important types of belief:

1. **A generalisation about a limit -**
   '£10,000 per month is the highest achievable sales performance'.
   'Four sales visits a day is the maximum possible.'

2. **A generalisation about the cause of something -**
   'Being an Entrepreneur means that Banks won't like me.
   'High quality training leads to high quality results'.

3. **A generalisation about the meaning -**
   'Average results means that I am average'.
   'Having a bad credit record means that I will not be able to raise much finance.'
   'Not having a good knowledge of selling means that my potential is limited'.

B – Why are beliefs important?

People with beliefs like the previous examples are unlikely to succeed. These beliefs need to be changed so that your behaviours will change in order to live up to the new regime. Behaviour is a function of the values, beliefs, needs and habits a person has. If you understand a person's values, beliefs, needs and habits, you will start seeing patterns. When you understand the patterns, you are in the inner workings of their behavioural impulses.

We often create our beliefs with insufficient information, as our mind automatically fills in the gaps. Once accepted, our beliefs become unquestioned commands to our nervous system, and they have the power to expand or destroy the possibilities of our present and future. Beliefs can be supportive in their effects or hold you back. Limiting beliefs usually have their root in strong negative experiences, often a single one in which the belief was formed. It is not the events themselves of our experiences that shape us, but our beliefs as to what those events mean.

A friend of mine, John, set himself up as a freelance consultant in his area of expertise. He believed strongly that he could not sell on the telephone. He would not even pick up the handset, always focusing on something else to do, which he knew in his heart was lower priority.

His wife tried to convince him that he was actually quite good, and that, as he could present and sell with confidence face-to-face, selling on the telephone was easier. They had many arguments back and forth. Some past experience must have had a very profound effect on him to convince him that he was no good on the phone. His wife became assertive and insisted that he call 20 people each day. He did so with her pressuring him, although he believed that he did not perform very well. Finally, she had an idea and said, 'Do all prospective customers tell lies about how they were influenced by a cold call from someone?' He thought about it and said, 'No, occasionally some might when it is in their interest to do so, but certainly not all.' So the wife said, 'Okay let us try an experiment. I will ring the twenty people I made you call this morning and record their comments. That way we can pick up with their tone what their real impression was.'

John thought that he had given a bad impression to all twenty, so was not particularly keen on this proposal, but he felt it would prove him right, so he agreed. His wife made the calls, in front of John, and recorded the conversations. Every reference was excellent, commending the caller on good manners, clarity of communication and professionalism. Feeling satisfied, the wife told her husband that here was proof that he in fact was a lot better at selling himself over the telephone than he thought.

John listened to the tapes in total disbelief. He put his pen down and said, 'I'll be damned, everybody does tell lies!'

The point of the story is that when you have a limiting belief, it will distort all new evidence, logic and argument until it fits. This is why belief is such an important area to peak performance. John does not need telephone technique training, he only needs to change his belief in his ability. It can have this effect positively or negatively. Positively is when you believe so strongly in the inevitability of your success that no amount of evidence to the contrary or setback will affect your commitment. Imagine that you had a belief so strong as to be a conviction that you could double your sales over the next six months. What do you think would happen?

C – The effect of beliefs on your selling

All of my commercial experience supports the following conviction: 'One person with the right beliefs will do far better than any of a thousand with better abilities and a keen interest, trying their best.' If you believe in your own success you will be empowered to achieve it.

If we make ten unsuccessful calls in a row, what will be the result of call eleven? Now, according to the 'numbers game' theory and mathematical logic, it should be like a roulette wheel. In other words, the outcome of each throw has no bearing on any other throw. In practice our previous experience sets us up with a belief that will strongly influence our subsequent performance.

Many of our beliefs are generalisations about our past, based on our interpretations of painful and pleasurable experiences. Often these beliefs are created by misinterpretation of past experiences. Once adopted, these beliefs, however incorrectly founded, become a part of your inner reality and assume a direct influence on your behaviour.

Whenever something happens to you whilst building your business, your mind will automatically ask: *'Is this good or bad news for me, and what must I do to encourage good news and avoid bad news in the future?'* You will then automatically form generalisations that determine your future behaviour. This is why so many people in their business avoid cold calling prospective customers. We make cold calls and experience failure and possibly unpleasantness from the recipient. This is bad news for us and we are then conditioned before the next call we make to expect failure and unpleasantness. How do you think we could break this cycle? Really think about this, as a solution that is produced by you will stand far more chance of success than my saying what works for me.

One person I know follows every call that goes well by writing the company name on a card in big letters, together with notes of what transpired, and sticking the card on the wall. The more calls he makes, the more cards go up on the wall. The more cards on the wall, the more he is reminded of his successes and his positive progress through the day. That breaks the bad-news cycle for him. What did you come up with?

If you find yourself saying, 'I cannot ...', ask yourself, 'What specifically stops me?' Sometimes people are able to produce outstanding results in difficult circumstances simply because they don't know the task in question is considered to be difficult.

> I once employed a trainee called Richard and he asked me how many telephone canvass calls I expected him to make each day in addition to his other work. I jokingly said a 100, but he took me seriously. At the end of the month I looked at his records and he had in fact made a 100 calls per day average. I had not thought that possible previously, and had never attempted it personally, nor expected staff to achieve this level. Imagine how popular Richard was from then on amongst his colleagues!

People may already have a lot of capabilities to influence their results, but if they don't believe they have those capabilities, they will probably fail to use them. Another point to consider is that the beliefs that others have about us will affect us. Telling the managers of two different yet comparable sales teams that their team is well above and well below average respectively has tested this. That belief of the manager is transmitted. Have you ever had a teacher, manager, parent who believed that you would have difficulty at something? I have observed in a large sales team that the top performer starts attracting a certain awe and respect. The others start believing that his figures are the highest achievable and aim towards them without really expecting to reach them. That is because 100% efficiency at anything is near impossible, (or is that perhaps just my limiting belief?). His figures certainly became their limiting belief.

People who have similar experiences may respond very differently. Many sales managers deal with the symptoms (average sales results, aversion to client visits, avoidance of cold calling). The cause in all of these cases could well be a limiting belief that is holding the representatives back. Alternatively it could simply be a lack of training and experience. Knowing which, is the challenge that separates average managers from the superb.

Here are some limiting beliefs that I have personally changed for clients.

Symptom	Possible Limiting Belief
Average sales results	• I am an average sales person. • I cannot do better because I don't have very good clients. • I have always performed at this level so I always will.
Aversion to client visits	• I am not very good at meeting people. • My gender is against me when I visit clients. • I need all the information at hand to give a good account of myself. • Clients on their home ground will be in a stronger position than me.
Avoidance of cold-calling	• I will be rejected on nearly every call. • Cold calling is always boring. • People hate being called by someone they don't know trying to sell them something. • If they wanted our products, they would ring.

D – Beliefs of top performers

The following questions are taken from a seminar I gave recently to a group of entrepreneurs and the self-employed.

- 'Who here believes that they *cannot* consistently be the top salesperson in their company? Hands up.'
- 'Who here believes that they *cannot* double their last six months' sales in the next six months? Hands up.'

The majority put their hands up. I then explained: 'If you put your hand up, all you have to do is replace those limiting beliefs with empowering ones, and your performance will significantly increase. Many entrepreneurs are trapped in their own past; it sets the limits for them.' A key belief for top performers is:

The past does not equal the future.

Progress now:

What is the one belief you could change right now that would make the biggest difference to your business? Write it below:

Sales superstars are distinguished by their beliefs. Here are a few examples:

Failure is feedback, which leads to learning and thus improvement. I know of a man who started a small business, worked all hours, despite advice from family and friends to get a regular job, and eventually, despite initial successes, went bankrupt. How did that affect him? What do you think his family and friends were telling him? What encouragement do you think he got from them to start another business? What financial support do you think he got from anyone? What do you think he did? He started another small business. What do you think happened to it? It went bust, that's what happened. Now, would you lend this guy money for a new venture? How do you think the banks reacted to him? Would you say that he was a gifted entrepreneur with a Midas touch? Shortly after his second bankruptcy he got into the motor trade in a small way. His name, Henry Ford! He used failure to learn, the more failure, the more learning. The more learning, the more success. Success, like beauty, is in the eye of the beholder. How do we know if we have succeeded or failed? Do we wait for someone to tell us or do we go and find out for ourselves? The answer perhaps is both, we examine our achievements ourselves, and we actively seek the views of others. Finding the right balance is the key.

If I look at my mistakes with reference to my objective and my other successes, then they are valuable feedback. As such I can learn and improve my future performance. Eventually, I am going to get all the results that I want – anything that gets in the way is feedback pointing me back on the right track.

- **Setting clear objectives with an equally clear timetable is essential.**
- **Planning long-term produces better results long-term.**
- **In every adversity is a hidden opportunity.**
- **Losing a deal means you are a loser, like eating carrots means you are a rabbit.**
- **I make it happen by taking action.**

Positive thinking alone is not enough – you need to take action. Things don't get better by themselves; they get better when somebody takes action. In a recession, or even during a boom in some instances, I have heard business people say, *'I can't wait until things get better'*, or *'I hope my current problems go away or I'm not going to make any deals'*. High achievers take the necessary appropriate actions to make things better. Problems that go away by themselves have a habit of coming back by themselves. If the situation is not working for you almost anything else you do is more appropriate.

- **Commitment is the key to excellence.**
- **Before my results change I have to change.**
- **Knowledge is only power when it is acted upon.**
- **Always give more than you expect to receive and you will receive more.**
- **I can go with flow of life or determine it.**

Successful people control their outstanding results because they make their own luck. Then average performers accuse them of being lucky.

- **Anything is possible.**
- **I alone am responsible for my results.**
- **Whatever someone else can achieve I am capable of doing much better.**
- **Limited beliefs create limited people.**
- **Your beliefs will expand or limit the beliefs of your client. If you believe that you are benefiting him, so will he.**
- **Belief in success is essential, techniques only help.**

Adopt these beliefs; paste them on the wall; constantly be reminded of them. You will adopt the beliefs of top sales superstars.

E – Supporting and limiting beliefs

Empowering beliefs examples:
- **I am capable of achieving everything that I want.**
- **I constantly seek to improve.**
- **Nobody has any advantages over me.**
- **I don't know it all. I can learn from everyone I meet.**

An attitude of constant and never-ending improvement will produce excellence. Think of a time recently that you made a sales presentation and it did not go as well as you would have wished. What could you have done differently? What did you learn from the experience? If you were in that situation tomorrow, what would you do differently?

Limiting beliefs examples

- ☒ I know it all.
- ☒ I am too old to learn new techniques.
- ☒ I can't....
- ☒ I don't....
- ☒ I'm no good at....

In my first position as a recruitment consultant, before I set up on my own, I asked the company's top performer the following question (annual figures were just out and he was personally responsible for £205,000 worth of invoices for permanent placements). *'What do you think is the highest possible placement figure you could achieve?'* He responded, *'Well, looking at it logically, taking into account all the various factors, the highest possible is about £135,000.'* He was then off talking to someone before I had a chance to ask him what he meant. Top achievers are not interested in what's 'possible', they are interested in what they want to achieve. What is 'possible' is a limiting belief as far as they are concerned and they do not waste valuable time with it. After Henry Ford went bust for the second time, did those around him consider it possible that he would build one of the world's biggest companies. What's 'possible' is an extremely limiting belief!

**Empowering beliefs + listening + knowing what to do +
taking action + feedback + flexibility = achievement of your goals**

Think of something that you want to do, but are holding back from because of past failure or concern. You are afraid that you might fail. If you knew that ultimately you would succeed, what would you attempt?

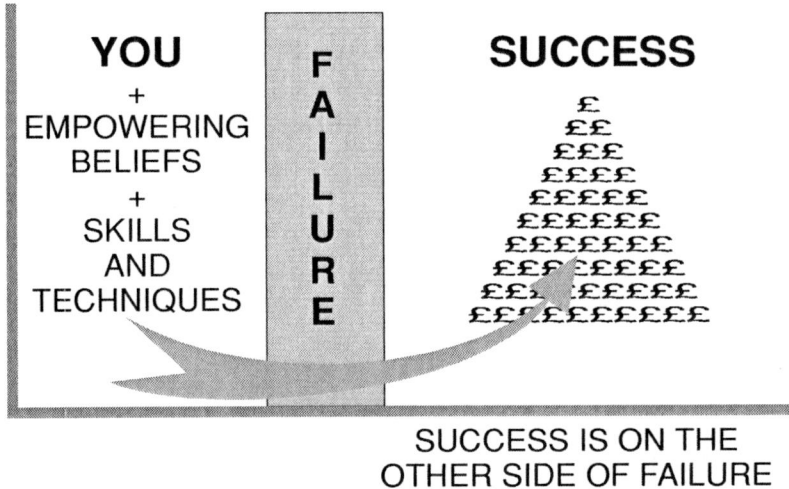

YOU + EMPOWERING BELIEFS + SKILLS AND TECHNIQUES — FAILURE — SUCCESS £ ££ £££ ££££ £££££ ££££££ £££££££ £££ ££££££ ££££ ££££££ ££££££££££

SUCCESS IS ON THE
OTHER SIDE OF FAILURE

F – How to make your beliefs supporting

Changing a limiting belief is like scoring a major deal. First you have to find a major customer, or in this case, find the limiting belief. In other words, establishing the limiting beliefs that are holding you back is easier said than done. This is because they can be buried deep in your subconscious and when they were being created, you were not consciously aware of it. Sometimes if we are lucky we may know our limiting beliefs.

Roger Bannister is famous for breaking the four-minute mile barrier. What is less known is that soon afterwards hundreds of people went on to achieve the same feat. Why do you think that was? When we believe something, by definition we stop questioning it. So how do you think we can start to change it? We question the validity of the belief. And if you question anything enough you will begin to doubt it, as contrary evidence mounts. What you are really doing is creating an alternative belief, which has a cancelling-out affect.

Ask these questions both to yourself and to colleagues and friends:

- What advantages do others have?
- What is my weakest attribute?
- What stops me from being the fastest growing company in my sector?
- What am I not the best at?

Amongst the answers to these questions you will find your limiting beliefs. It is usually easier to do this exercise in pairs; and remember that when we are talking about limiting and supporting beliefs, it is of no interest whether they are true or not. If you believe them they are true for you.

Most major improvements in sales performance, in my experience, begin with a change in beliefs. The easiest way to change a belief is to associate substantial 'bad news' with the old belief.

- Create doubt by questioning.
- Think of exceptions to the old belief.
- Apply Verbal Aikido (see later) to look at the belief from a different perspective.

What we want to do now is collect as much evidence as possible to contradict the limiting belief and to support a new empowering one. So make these challenges to your limiting beliefs.

- How is this belief ridiculous or absurd?
- Do the leaders in my sector hold this belief?
- What will it cost me to keep this belief?
- Can I think of any clear exceptions to the belief?
- What caused me to have this belief in the first place? Do the assumptions still hold?

Now we replace the old belief with a new empowering belief, by finding as many reasons with as much evidence as possible to support the new belief. To help create and develop your empowering beliefs, ask yourself.

- What evidence supports this belief?
- When have I known it to be true?
- Who do I know who has this belief?
- Why do they believe it?
- Do the successful entrepreneurs I know hold this belief?
- What would happen if I firmly held this belief?

G – A belief-change exercise

The following is the abridged transcript of a coaching exercise I performed for a client who wanted more empowering beliefs. It provides a good example of the way that you can go about changing your own beliefs. (See below, to apply the process to your own beliefs)

Alex: List three beliefs you have, first limiting and second supporting your performance.

Client: *Limiting beliefs*
1. £10,000 is the maximum sales I could possible achieve in a month.
2. I am below average at cold calling and hate it.
3. The competition has clear advantages over us.
Supporting beliefs
1. I can maintain enthusiasm and drive after a setback.
2. People like me.
3. I sincerely care about my customer's best interests.

Alex: Now look at the three limiting beliefs listed, and list three beliefs that you would prefer to have.

Client: 1. Whatever result I can achieve, I can do 10% better the following month.
2. I am exceptionally talented at cold calling and love it.
3. Whatever resources the competition has it is no match for my determination, dedication and enthusiasm.

Alex: *(referring to the first limiting belief, '£10,000 is the maximum sales I could possible do in a month.')*: Tell me in your own words everything that is ridiculous or absurd about this belief?

Client: Uh, well, nothing, that's why I believe it. *(Eyes move up and to the left, indicating that he is accessing visual memories, explained more in later chapter.)*

Alex: If you could see something absurd about it, what would that be?

Client: Well, I suppose that so many things could change making it easier to achieve... and therefore it is ridiculous in a way.

Alex: What kind of things?

Client: You know, inflation could make it easier.

Alex: What else?

Client: Lots of things.

Alex: Go on.

Client: A major competitor goes bust, if we had better marketing, a better corporate web page would help. (Eyes now going to the right side indicating to me he was constructing ideas.)

Alex: What else could change?

Client: If I changed my belief. Ha, Ha.

Alex: So you are happy to accept that if you can change your belief, then you already have the requisite abilities to exceed £10,000 per month.

Client: I suppose so.

Alex: What else could change?

Client: Well, if I had more confidence in my own abilities.

Alex: How could your confidence be improved?

Client: Well, if I exceeded £10,000 per month it would automatically go up.

Alex: Okay. To get around that catch 22, let us pretend. I want you to close your eyes and imagine that last month you did £12,000 worth of personal sales into the business. Imagine your staff talking to you, what would they be saying? What would you be saying? What would it feel like?

Now, bearing in mind that our brain's circuits are the same for imagining fiction as for reality, using imagination in this way can be a very powerful tool. As long as I can persuade the client to make the experience as vivid as possible the effect will be as though it were true. I continue to do this by talking him through all the internal sensory experience, i.e. using visual, auditory and feeling languages, and we return to the interview a little later ...

Alex: Now, how do you feel now about doing £12,000 next month? Do you think you can do it?

Client: Well, I'll give it my best shot.

Alex: *(Now, we are clearly not there yet, but we are in a better position than when we started).* What else can be done to increase your confidence?

Client:	Praise. I'd like my boss and my peers to tell me how well I did sometimes, this may sound stupid but it builds me up.
Alex:	Okay, so what could you do to get them to do that?
Client:	I never thought that I could influence it. Ask them I suppose, after all, we have a team commission structure. But I think they will laugh.
Alex:	What else could change?
Client:	I don't know.
Alex:	Who do you think might know?
Client:	My wife always has good ideas with this sort of thing.
Alex:	Okay. If she were here now sitting over there, what do you think she would say?
Client:	That if I didn't keep avoiding cold calling with feeble excuses, I would have a bigger database to pitch to.
Alex:	Okay. How exactly do you avoid cold calling?
Client:	Well, I just avoid it.
Alex:	No, I mean exactly. If I had to step in for you tomorrow, how would I go about avoiding cold calling.
Client:	Well, I imagine the people getting angry and not responding to what I say. *(His face drops, his tone lowers and his voice slows to a drawl.)*
Alex:	Okay. What do you think you could do to change that?
Client:	Go on a training course I suppose.
Alex:	Okay, why don't you pursue that idea … Now, let us sum up where we have got to, so far. You think your limiting belief is absurd because:

- many things could change
- inflation could erode the value
- a competitor could go bust
- you could gain more confidence
- you received training in cold calling.

That limiting belief is looking pretty silly isn't it?

Client:	Yes, I see what you mean …

In the transcript above, I have only gone through the first challenging question, in order to demonstrate the idea. Clearly, by the time the other questions are exhausted, the belief is all but gone. Note that if you are working in pairs, it is important that the person being worked on comes up with their own solutions. Try not to make solutions and suggestions for them. The solutions have got to be produced and accepted by their unconscious mind in order for change to occur at a deep level. Now let us turn to helping the client create the first empowering belief that he would like to create: 'Whatever result I can achieve, I can do 10% better the following month …'

Alex: Do you know of anyone with that belief?

Client: Let me think …Ah yes, Peter seems to take that attitude.

Alex: Okay. What did you think led him to that belief?

Client: Well, Peter thinks that there is no substitute for experience and that every day of every month there are lessons to be learnt. Therefore at the start of each following month he believes he is older and wiser and therefore works that little bit better. And in sales a marginal deal can mean a lot on the sales figures.

Alex: What else do you think has led him to this belief?

Client: I don't really know, but the more I think about it the more I am convinced that he does have this belief that I would like. But I still believe that there is a limit to the number of calls you can make, the number of clients you can visit. etc, and at the end of the day everybody reaches their own plateau.

Alex: Have you asked Peter himself about the belief?

Client: No, but I am certainly going to now that I have thought of it.

Alex: What determines your plateau level?

Client: The sales target, I guess.

Alex: And has there ever been a time when you exceeded it?

H – Your turn to change your beliefs

Write on the following pages your limiting and supporting beliefs and also the beliefs you would like to replace the limiting beliefs with. Then answer the following questions, challenging each limiting belief and supporting the empowering belief that you want to change it with. I have also included questions on your present empowering beliefs, although these are not worked on specifically. Their purpose is to help establish your strengths, to help your thinking about beliefs process, to provide a basis for comparison between your current limiting and supporting beliefs. This is to provide you with a final list of six empowering beliefs, which should be stuck up on the wall in your office for reinforcement.

Progress now:

Defining current and desired beliefs

List 3 beliefs you have both supporting and limiting.

LIMITING BELIEFS

1.

2.

3.

SUPPORTING BELIEFS

1.

2.

3.

Now list 3 empowering beliefs you would like to acquire.

PREFERRED EMPOWERING BELIEFS

1.

2.

3.

To challenge a limiting belief, ask the following questions.

- What examples can I think of when this belief was not true or did not apply?

- In what way is this belief ridiculous or absurd?

- Do the top sales people in my company hold this belief?

- What will it cost me to keep this belief?

- What exceptions are there to the belief?

- What caused me to have the belief in the first place? And do the assumptions still hold?

Creating and developing the empowering belief

Ask the following questions of the belief you want to create.

- What evidence supports this belief?

- When have I known it to be true?

- Who do I know who has this belief?

- Do the top sales people I know hold this belief?

- What will happen when I hold this belief?

I – Group belief change

A company I visited recently had six sales staff who had just spent the last two weeks agreeing targets with their Sales Director. The total target was £600,000, comprising individual targets between £60,000 and £135,000. Initially the individuals had come up with their own figures totalling £420,000. The Sales Director got this figure up while maintaining agreement that they could do it. He knew that cooperation was essential for a target to be meaningful.

Having been invited to make a presentation, I asked about their new annual targets. I wrote the individual and total figures on a board. I then said, 'I want you to imagine that I have planted an electrical device on you and your loved ones. If these figures are not at least doubled by this time next year I will pull the switch and you and your loved ones will all receive a painful jolt. Believing this without any doubts, who thinks that they will do it?' Six hands shot up. You just need to access those resources you have without the need for negative motivation.

I continued: 'What exactly can you do, that you are not doing now, that will enable you to accomplish this? What changes would have to be made? What changes would you risk trying?'

I then said, 'Imagine it is a year from now. I have returned and we are all drinking champagne celebrating this marvellous achievement. From this perspective looking back, what was it that you did that empowered you to produce these results?' During the course of the afternoon the Sales Director could not believe the excited conversations, ideas and creativity that was coming forth from his staff. He was delighted with the result.

If you are determined, the belief change system outlined in this chapter will work and will lead to significant improvements in your results.

5

Peak Performance Selling

'I shall never surrender or retreat.'
William Travis, Commander of the Alamo

'Sometimes it is not good enough to do your best;
you have to do what's required.'
Sir Winston Churchill

This chapter ...

A   The Success Index
B   Getting into our peak performance state
C   The importance of state of mind
D   Peak health
E   The highs and lows
F   The success cycle
G   How you can create unstoppable self-confidence
H   The keys to your performance level
I   Turning the keys

A – The Success Index

Do the following attitudes and beliefs apply to you?

yes/no

1. My confidence is unshakeable.

2. I am committed to constant and never-ending improvement.

3. I am resourceful and have the ability to do whatever it takes to succeed.

4. I see problems as challenges and react to them positively.

5. I have tremendous confidence in my talents and abilities.

6. I control my results.

7. I am committed to excellence.

8. Whatever my results are, I can improve them.

9. I am a 'do it now' person and manage my time well.

10. I am eager to get into action as I wake up each day.

11. I know exactly what I want to achieve.

12. I learn by my mistakes. I look at failure as feedback for improvement.

13. I control my emotional state not external events.

14. I eat and drink healthily.

15. I exercise regularly and sleep well.

16. I nearly always have an abundance of energy.

17. I believe that whatever results somebody else can get I can achieve to.

18. I love cold calling and look forward to telling new people about my business.

19. I set daily outcomes.

20. I respect my competitors and learn from them.

yes/no

21. When I meet someone, I make my impression of them by how they come across (dress, body language, voice tone), rather than the specific things they say.

22. I expect to win the business when I visit a client.

23. I am constantly asking myself, 'what can I do to be a little better?'

24. I know how to use my physiology to control my state of mind.

25. I vary my approach to each client.

26. If what I am doing is not getting the desired result, I experiment and try alternatives.

27. I know that my confidence and passion in my business is so strong it is contagious and itself convinces clients to use us.

28. I am not held back by a fear of rejection.

29. Any resource a competitor has is nothing compared to my creativity, ability, enthusiasm and skill.

30. I can think of thirty benefits of a customer choosing my business.

31. I am confident speaker and presenter when the need arises.

32. If I make ten unsuccessful cold calls in a row it will not affect my confidence for call eleven.

33. I rarely start sentences with 'I can't....'

34. I know how to use questions to direct my own mental focus.

35. I am an outstanding sales person for my business.

36. Belief in success is essential, techniques only help.

37. I can maintain enthusiasm and drive after a setback.

38. I am a really good listener and miss little.

39. I am confident that I can develop rapport with anybody.

40. If a potential client said that our competitors were offering a lower price, it wouldn't make me drop mine.

	yes/no
41. If I don't get it right at first, I will keep trying.	
42. We offer a much better overall deal than our competitors.	
43. There is no such thing as a difficult customer.	
44. Whatever obstacle I come up against there is always a way through, I just have to find it.	
45. I visualise a successful outcome before every sales call/visit.	
46. I have a clear written business and sales plan and refer to it regularly.	
47. I think of our competitors as coaches.	
48. Whatever happens there is always good news in it somewhere.	
49. Our main competitors will never be as good as we are.	
50. I can tell what sort of a mood someone is in just by the way they answer the telephone.	

Calculate your percentage of 'yes' responses. This represents your efficiency in using your current abilities. It also highlights the areas that need attention. A score of 70% means that your performance can be improved by 30% by improving confidence and beliefs alone!

If you got a 100% ask a friend to complete it again for you!

Now highlight each 'no' answer and write it on a separate piece of paper. Write in the following question: 'What can I do to change this to yes?'

B – Getting into our peak performance state

What sort of month have you had?

GREAT	OH DEAR
Smiling	Frowning
Head up	Head down
Shoulders up	Shoulders rounded
Firm stride	Slow walk
Talks Fast	Drawls
Positive words	Negative words
Excited	Depressed
Enthusiasm	Boredom
Looking up	Looking down

Our first communication is to ourselves!

C – The importance of state of mind

Richard had set himself up as a freelance Executive Recruitment Consultant and was on his way to a presentation with a potentially major account. His secretary called him on his mobile telephone.

'Hi, Richard – Mary here. Great news, the company you visited yesterday are moving their entire account to us. That will make them our largest customer. Well done, incredible, we'll open some champagne on your return.'

How well do you think Richard will do at his imminent presentation?

Ten minutes later, while parking, Richard's telephone rings again. 'Richard, bad news, I'm afraid. Their FD has just rung and said that as we are relatively small, we are vulnerable and they cannot risk placing their entire account with us. They apologise for telling us otherwise. Could you call in on them before returning and see if you can do anything?'

Now how well do you think Richard will do at his imminent presentation?

Same person, same experience, same knowledge, same abilities, etc, but his performance level can be changed in an instant. Lack of control of 'emotional state' loses more sales than lack of technique, experience or ability. Let us assume that Richard is passionate about his services and knows how to make a good presentation. He controls his 'peak performance state' as follows.

Before every customer visit, he visualises his best ever presentation, he sees, hears and feels it vividly as though it was happening now. This concentration clears out all other thoughts and gets him into a dynamic state for the presentation. All his resources are focused on the job in hand. He then walks in and gets the business.

Successful people then, are those that are able to gain consistent access to their most resourceful states. When we create the appropriate 'state of mind', we create the greatest possible chance for using all our faculties effectively.

Your behaviour is created by your state, which in turn is determined by your body language, which again can be changed in minutes. You can completely control your 'state of mind' and thus performance level by ensuring your whole physiology (body language) is vibrant, dynamic, motivated and positive. You can control your physiology by being healthy, which will create vitality, energy and enthusiasm. Health in turn is created by a balanced combination of exercise and a nutritious diet. It is a circle that can be used to support you. Be careful though, if the circle is overheated, stress can sneak in, which can equally work around the circle destroying all the good work.

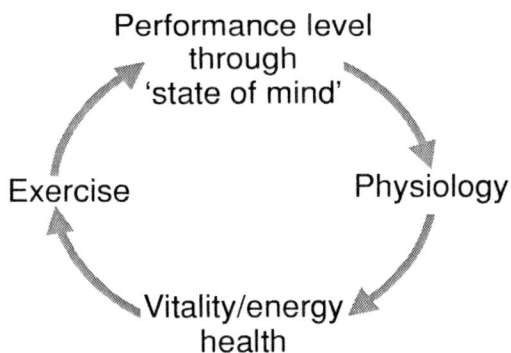

Performance level
through
'state of mind'

Exercise   Physiology

Vitality/energy
health

Figure 2 – The Circle of Success

So at what point do you start on the 'circle of success'? Imagine you have to go for an interview or presentation today; how do you feel about it? The first thoughts and images that go through your mind as you imagine this should indicate your current state of mind, and from this you can determine your own start point on the circle.

Experience and reading of biographies has shown me that nearly all highly successful entrepreneurs have vivid imaginations. They see it, feel it, hear it, and thoroughly experience it in their mind before they go ahead. They begin with an exact knowledge of what they intend to achieve before they actually do it. When they get into the real situation, it does not scare them, because there is no unknown. They are confident, and through that confidence and mental preparation they are able to influence the way events turn out, and steer the events along their own preconceived routes. There's something rather amazing about what happens when you get a clear internal representation of what you want. It programmes your mind and body to achieve that goal.

You need to visualise a success in order to programme yourself to achieve it. Conversely, if you visualise failure you programme yourself to achieve it. Think now about going to visit the hardest, most unpleasant person in the world in the next five minutes to sell him something. What images immediately pop into your mind? If they are images of failure change them to images of success. Run through some images in your mind of everything going well. Notice how you have already changed the way that you think about the meeting.

If you take a moment to notice people walking down a street, their body language will give away what state of mind, or mood they are in. The speed alone is usually an accurate indicator, depressed people walk slowly, excited and enthusiastic people walk fast. If you can do this, so can people you visit.

A suggestion – park away from clients when visiting and have a ten-minute brisk walk to their office. Remain standing in reception. Constantly check the relationship between your state, internal thoughts, physiology and results.

D – Peak health

The mind and body are two parts of the same system. They work in unison and have a direct effect on each other. Neither of them can operate independently. The mind works at its best when the body is in a healthy, positive state. Wise entrepreneurs keep very fit! They exercise regularly, eat nutritious foods and avoid late nights. I attend my local Karate club regularly – I even interviewed the owner for my previous book. Interestingly, I found that a large number of the adults attending regularly were also successful entrepreneurs of some description. Karate gives them discipline, focus and energy, as would many other sports. That makes them strong and resourceful and helps them to feel good and positive about themselves. When we feel resourceful in this way, we will attempt things that we would not normally attempt, and succeed at them.

Keeping healthy habits is an excellent start and an essential foundation for a successful state of mind. With this foundation in place, we can move on more effectively to the exercise of visualising successful outcomes (see previous section). Visualising confidence, success and peak performance will be made far easier the fitter, stronger and healthier you feel. This is what Olympic athletes do before the race. They run a movie in their minds of themselves winning their event – imagining victory, or perhaps recalling a recent event in which they excelled. They combine fitness and visualisation techniques to help them achieve.

Throughout the working day, things happen and we react to them, changing our mental 'state' as we do so. The trick is to provide your own stimuli (run a movie in your mind of your greatest achievement) and thus control your emotional 'state'. I have noticed time and time again in small business that the real winners are the ones who can think positively and bounce back, even after a succession of rejections or setbacks, often even more determined than before. You now know how they do it and you can too. Most people, on the other hand, slow down and question their ability and skill, which in turn erodes their confidence. Hence the 'vicious circle'. They then lose the next deal.

As the body and mind are totally related, anything less than peak fitness can only hold you back from your potential.

Progress now:

Answer the following questions:

● What can I change to eat more healthily?

● What can I change to drink more healthily?

● What can I change to get more from exercise?

● What will be the effect of the above changes on my performance?

What you eat, drink and think determines your results.

E – The highs and lows

Progress now:

- What was your worst selling experience ever?

- What was your most successful selling experience?

- What is the difference in how you 'code' these memories?

1 - How did you think when you succeeded?

What did you see?

What did you feel?

What did you hear?

2 - How did you think when you failed?

What did you see?

What did you feel?

What did you hear?

---

3 - *What is the key difference between success and failure?*

What did you see differently between 1 and 2?

What did you feel differently between 1 and 2?

What did you hear differently between 1 and 2?

4 - *What happens when you think about your failures in the same way that you think about your successes? How does it affect the feelings? What learning does this offer you?*

Most people find that they code 'success' and 'failure' in a completely different way. If you think in 'success' mode, this will help you to establish the expectation of success in your mind; your brain will then automatically adjust your behaviours to keep you on target to your new expectation. The answers to the above questions will provide your success keys when you think about a sales presentation coming up. Force yourself to see, hear and feel it according to your personal success keys. This will ensure that you are in your most resourceful state.

F – The success cycle

Progress now:

Describe in detail your four greatest successes over the last year:

(a) describe what happened
(b) how you excelled
(c) what it felt like
(d) the positive things you told yourself and heard from others
(e) how things looked to you at this time.

(continued)

---

1. (a)

    (b)

    (c)

    (d)

    (e)

2. (a)

    (b)

    (c)

    (d)

    (e)

3. (a)

    (b)

    (c)

    (d)

    (e)

4. (a)

    (b)

    (c)

    (d)

    (e)

Read through these success records daily to uplift your confidence.

When our confidence goes up, it inspires us to take action. The more action we take, the greater our results. Greater results create greater beliefs in our abilities, skills, potential and so on. The more empowering our beliefs, the greater our confidence becomes. This cycle can be triggered off from any start point.

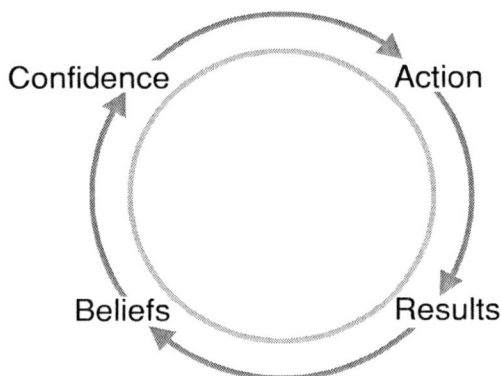

Figure 3 – The Success Cycle

The converse is also true. After a bad result, a rejection or setback, our beliefs as to our abilities tend to be challenged. We ask ourselves negative questions like, 'Why does it always happen to me? Why can't I get it right?' These questions get answers which erode our supporting beliefs, replacing them with holding-back beliefs. For example: 'However hard I try, I can never break the £10,000 of sales a month barrier; it just isn't possible for me.' Down goes the confidence. Due to low confidence, we feel less inclined and motivated to take action, and so it goes on if we let it. Eventually something happens to reverse the process.

The average person is constantly having 'good runs' and 'bad runs'. The winner who makes the breakthroughs has learnt how to maintain his personal success cycle. As soon as he senses something slowing down, he corrects it and maintains his peak performance state. The first thing then is to notice the point of change from a good towards a bad run. The second thing is to increase any of the four critical parts of the success cycle. Some top performers just 'get their head down' and take non-stop action. Some use visualisation or a physiological change to get their confidence up. Going for a brisk walk or a tough work-out in a gym can be enough. Some read through their success and reaffirm their supporting beliefs. Most, however, wait for a lucky result to pick them up. This is the worst one to pick because results depend upon action being taken first, and while they are waiting, confidence and belief diminish.

Progress now:

Referring to your four great successes, at what point did your Success Cycle start?

1.

2.

3.

4.

G – How you can create unstoppable self-confidence

Many things can bring down your self-confidence if you let them when you are in business for yourself. Friends and family can actually be the greatest demotivators whilst trying to be helpful. What about the uncertainty, the risk, the mortgage, they say. Are you sure there is a market for your ideas. These can all be good points, but they can be said in a way that, because they are close to you, erodes your self-confidence. You will be amazed how many of them will regularly offer expert opinion and advice without the backing of a day of experience. If you want advice on anything, my advice is to ask those that have been there and done it. If you have to take criticism personally let it spur you into action.

A confident state leads to target-busting results.

'Great State' = 'Great Results'
So how can we develop an unstoppable confidence?

Answer 1: *Change your physiology radically.*
   ● Go for a run or brisk walk.

- Take a break.
- Do some exercise.
- Stand tall, breathe deeply, smile and look up.
- Tell a joke and enjoy a good laugh.

Answer 2: *Control your mental focus.*
- Expect the best to happen.

What are you picturing, hearing, and feeling in your mind? How do you do that differently for a resourceful or a depressed state? What are the 'keys' that will make your state instantly resourceful? Direct your mind to success with the right questions.

> *'How can I turn this to advantage?'*
> *'What's the best way to achieve my objective?'*
> *'What opportunities are there here?'*

The questions we ask ourselves have a direct influence on our state of mind. The answers are our evaluations. If we ask, *'Why does it always go wrong for me?'* we will find an answer: *'Because I am no good, I just can't do it.'* This evaluation will depress us. Our state of mind is a result of the questions we ask.

My favourite way of getting into a resourceful state is a brisk walk around the local area while concentrating on questions that direct me to what I wish to achieve.

Progress now:

When you are in your *failure state,* what are the questions you ask yourself?

When you are in your *success state,* what are the questions you ask yourself (and what are the answers)?

Ask other people why they are brilliant at something. Notice how this clearly uplifts their state of mind. All I am asking you to do is ask yourself the same questions regularly.

H – The keys to your performance level

I would now like you to do the following exercise, which will establish how you personally prepare yourself for success and failure. This exercise is best done with a friend in a quiet place where you will not be disturbed and which supports concentration. Take turns asking each other the following questions. First you must elicit the desired state and not just interrogate the other person on it.

1. Tell them to think of a time (closing their eyes if helps) when they were incredibly successful. Tell them to imagine they are there now, enjoying that incredible success ... Continue talking them into this 'success state' until their facial expression indicates to you that they are there and not just saying it. Saying I have got a 'successful state' with a depressed look on the face is not convincing.
2. Now ask them to describe their internal experience in their own words. Ask them to describe what they see, hear and feel. Record this information on the form set out below.
3. Repeat steps 1 and 2 for their 'failure state'.
4. Ascertain what the critical differences are between the two experiences. Do this by your own judgement and reference to your notes and confirm by asking them.
5. Now take the 'failure' and get them to think about it in the same way as they do for a success. For example, let us say for a success they visualise colourful panoramic pictures, with loud voices of people telling them pleasant things. For a failure they visualise tiny black and white pictures with people murmuring behind their back about how incompetent they are. In this case, you say: 'Right, with the failure in mind imagine you have a TV remote controller. I want you now to turn the colour up until the picture is quite attractive. Now I would like you to enlarge the picture until it is all around you. Then change those voices to pleasant things and turn up the volume.'
6. Now ask them how they react to the 'failure' – how does it seem to them

now? When you can clearly see that their physiology (body language) is the same as it was for their 'successful state' you have got their success key. This key is immensely valuable. They now know how to access their peak performance state at will, whatever the setback.

	Success	Failure
PICTURES		
Through own eyes or		
like watching a movie	_____	_____
Location	_____	_____
Distance	_____	_____
Brightness	_____	_____
Colour	_____	_____
Size	_____	_____
Clarity	_____	_____
Movement	_____	_____
Speed	_____	_____
Depth	_____	_____
Duration	_____	_____
Frame/Panorama	_____	_____
SOUNDS		
Inside/Outside	_____	_____
Location	_____	_____
Distance	_____	_____
Clarity	_____	_____
Speed	_____	_____
Continuous	_____	_____
Volume	_____	_____
Tone	_____	_____
Words/Sounds	_____	_____
Whose Voice	_____	_____
Mono/Stereo	_____	_____
Duration	_____	_____
FEELINGS		
Location	_____	_____
Extent	_____	_____
Shape	_____	_____

Pressure	_____	_____
Temperature	_____	_____
Movement	_____	_____
Duration	_____	_____
Frequency	_____	_____
Intensity	_____	_____
Texture	_____	_____

I – Turning the keys

Now we know our keys, how can we use them to open the door to success?

1. Correct 'low' states immediately

- When you notice that you are 'low' correct it.
- Start thinking about the 'problem' with your success keys.
- See success, hear success and feel success.
- Adopt your physiology for success, stance, posture, breathing, facial expression, movement.
- Ask results-orientated questions.

2. Prepare For Action

How do we business owners feel before a cold-calling session or perhaps a client visit? We sometimes have a problem with cold calling, not because of lack of technique but how we 'set ourselves up' before calling. We picture aggressive prospects with loud voices telling us not to bother them. This belief in failure is transmitted through voice tone. Then, guess what? We fail. Then guess what? We tell ourselves: 'See – I knew it was going to be difficult (Recognise the cycle?).

3. Take Action!

6

Motivation Magic

'Never give in! Never give in! Never, never, never, never in nothing great or small, large or petty.'

Winston Churchill

'It is all very well and good knowing your product, and making a good presentation, but unless you connect at an emotional level, you will not consistently win good business. People buy from people, you have to make them feel passionate about what you offer.'

Kevin Uphill

'A mediocre idea that generates enthusiasm will go farther than a great idea that inspires no one.'

Mary Kay Ash

This chapter ...

A The power of negative thinking
B Motivation - avoiding bad news, seeking good news
C Morning focus
D Setting up your 'Motivation Magic' switch
E The Points Award Self-Motivation Scheme (PAS)
F If you find yourself reticent to call strangers
G Getting to and keeping at ten
H Always make one more call
I Public speaking

A – Harnessing the power of negative thinking

I once gave a lecture on motivation and put a flip chart on both the left and right hand side of the front of the class. I asked the group to write everything on the right flip chart that motivated them positively. I asked for things on the left hand flip chart that motivated them negatively, i.e. things they wanted to avoid.

After 20 minutes, ten pages on the negative board were used up and the positive board had not filled one half of a page.

If I said you can have one hour of everything pleasant you could possibly imagine in return for 5 minutes of experiencing everything negative you could possibly imagine, what would you say. Well, I have found that few people will take the offer. This suggests that keeping away from unpleasant things is more than ten times as powerful a human motivator as moving towards the goals of things we like. Puts a whole different perspective on achieving goals doesn't it?

There are hundreds of books on positive thinking, but how many of them radically improve the lives of the readers. Not many, because negative thinking is ten times more motivational that its positive counterpart. People are told the benefits of eating fresh fruit and vegetables and doing regular exercise. Do they do it? No. If they then have a mild heart attack, would they then change their attitude to healthy living? Yes, you bet they would. Fear of that negative experience happening again moves them to take action. Whatever it is, usually negative motivation works faster and stronger. The personal development industry for years has filled the shelves in bookshops and delegates into training courses with advice on positive thinking. 'Think positive' has become the mantra of business. Sounds great, sounds logical – it just does not work that effectively.

Researching this topic, I have read in great detail, reading very much between the lines, the biographies of famous entrepreneurs. I also read the biographies of other famous people to learn their secrets. The interesting thing I noted is that people who are successful at something don't do it the way most textbooks tell you to. The theory and the practice are worlds apart. I suggest you read some biographies yourself of people you wish to learn from and look between the lines to establish what really motivated them.

I have an audio product project underway at the time of writing with the above title, *'Harnessing the Power of Negative Thinking'*. I have already improved company results by teaching people how to practically use negative motivation to increase results. I have researched very successful people, specifically entrepreneurs. There is no doubt in my mind that negative thinking beats positive thinking in achieving success.

So think negatively – start by anticipating future threats and take measures to avert them now, whilst time is still an ally. Not when they become real and time has become the enemy. For example, think of what you can do if the following happens and decide a policy and action plan now, and put things in place. I know so many people who learnt about the importance of backing up their computer files through having their files corrupted.

1. Cash flow crisis *(Get a credit line available now when you don't need it. They will be less available to you when you do).*
2. Your best customer closes down *(Make sure you do not have too much business exposed at any one customer).*
3. A key member of staff resigns *(Do things to keep them loyal and locked in now).*
4. Your web site crashes *(Have a contingency plan or a second web site ready).*
5. All your computer files are hit by a virus *(Back up at the end of each day).*
6. A Recession hits your market *(Ask yourself ahead of time how can you can profit from this).*

Action overcomes fear by moving you away from it. Negative thinking means making mental pictures, sounds and feelings of what failure would be like. Then each day move as far away from these as you can. They will drive you 24/7, they will push you to go that extra mile. Not being able to bear the idea of coming second will push you further than the pull of wanting to come first. Churchill imagined what England would be like under the Third Reich. These images and thoughts were so horrible that no cost was not worth paying to stop it. That is how we won the Battle of Britain – many of our pilots were Czechs and Poles and had real images in their mind of what life was like under the Third Reich.

Progress now:

> Design a way that you can motivate *yourself* negatively: For example with a previous male business partner, we did the following. We agreed that if we did not hit the week's sales target, we would have to go to the pub on a Friday night and order two babychams!
>
> Believe me. It never happened, and it won't.
>
> Now your turn.

Progress now:

> Design a way that you can motivate *your staff* negatively.

B – Motivation – avoiding bad news, seeking good news

Are you motivated by avoiding bad news or seeking good news? In other words, is your motivation style based upon moving away from threats or towards rewards, moving away from the stick or towards the carrot? Most people are somewhere between the two with the average as we have seen being far nearer to the stick. It is important to have some idea where, as this will determine where the emphasis should be for you when motivating yourself.

For example, let us say that you want to make fifty telephone canvass calls a day. However, somewhere along the way your motivation wanes and you never consistently perform the task as well as you would like. Typically, nine out of ten calls don't produce a result. Therefore being rejected nine times (bad news) outweighs being accepted once (good news). To avoid bad news you therefore avoid cold calling.

How can you allocate more bad news to not doing the calls and good news to doing them? **The answer is to allocate as much 'bad news' as possible to not doing them and as much 'good news' as possible to doing them. Obvious, really!**

Bad news if you don't do the calls

- ☒ no future clients
- ☒ less opportunity to build the business
- ☒ miss opportunities that were just waiting for the picking
- ☒ beaten by competition
- ☒ go bankrupt
- ☒ constant nagging pressure and guilt from not doing it
- ☒ limited client base
- ☒ declining size of client base
- ☒ less interesting work to do.

Good news if you do the calls

- ☑ business grows faster
- ☑ plenty of potential customers
- ☑ breakthrough sales to a new level
- ☑ feedback information on market conditions
- ☑ satisfaction of success
- ☑ money (list all the things that you want money for)
- ☑ new car
- ☑ every ten calls means a result thus each call is 10% success
- ☑ leads to securing the business
- ☑ sooner done, the quicker you can move on.

Progress now:

Compile your own lists, and when you have completed them as thoroughly as you can, read them and think about them before every canvassing session.

C – Morning focus

Start the day as you mean to go on. Every morning, ask yourself five questions that will get you into a resourceful state, focusing on achievement for the day. When you have decided on your five questions, stick them on a wall so that you see them before you leave home in the morning.

Answer these questions every morning. Put them in a prominent place, where you will see them soon after waking up. They will immediately get your mind focused towards your objectives and provide you with a positive orientation.

1. What do I wish to achieve today?

2. Who would be really worth calling or e-mailing?

3. What could I do today that is different and useful?

4. What would make me happy if I achieved it today? What can I do to achieve it?

5. What would I have done differently yesterday if I had the chance?

Progress now:

What are the three most powerful questions that you can ask yourself in order to access your most resourceful state?

1.

2.

3.

D – Setting up your 'Motivation Magic' switch

When you are ready to be geared up for your motivation magic state, wouldn't it be nice to be able to access it just by flicking a switch that immediately opens it up? Well, if we think about it, there are various naturally occurring 'switches'. For example, when I listen to an old Beatles hit, it immediately takes me back to my teenage days to where I was living, what I was doing and the people around me at that time. It is a very nostalgic experience. In fact, for me, and for most people. I suspect, hearing any pop music hit, particularly if I really liked the group, takes me back to the experiences that I was having when it was in the charts. Do you have a piece of favourite music that takes you to a time when you were unstoppable? Other memories can also affect my 'state' immediately, usually something involving high emotional content whether it is good or bad news.

Now the question is, if these strong links occur naturally, how can we harness that power to enable us to access our most resourceful, peak performance states when we need them? When we are naturally in our peak performance state, I mean really feeling good, we should introduce a stimulus at the height of the feeling, clench a fist, shout, 'Yes, Yes, Yes', play our favourite music ... whatever. In fact, I have found that for most people certain music will already have strong emotions for them and uplift their state – for example, Land Of Hope And Glory, Chariots Of Fire, the theme to Rocky, Simply The Best, or the theme to 'The Dambusters'.

Of course, as well as controlling your own emotional states, you will also want to influence the 'state' of the recipient of your communication. For example, if you want a future client in a buying state, ask him about a time when he bought the type of product you are selling and ask him as much as possible about it. While you are gaining information about how he buys and what is important for him, he is reliving a successful purchase and cannot help but access his 'buying state'.

E – The Points Award Self-motivation scheme (PAS)

What is PAS? It is an incentive programme designed to motivate people both on an individual and a team basis. It also allows you to monitor and review your own performance and have a useful yardstick from which to improve. The basic theme is: 'Never try to be better than someone else; be better than yourself'. It is therefore very applicable to those who are self-employed and entrepreneurs who have no boss. PAS gives you the feedback that indicates where you can improve and what you have to do. Although you will want to know what other people are achieving, the important thing to remember is to constantly improve on your own performance.

Traditionally, building a reputation and a database of customers takes time. Often, when a client places an order, it follows a period of selling activity over a number of weeks. Therefore, good work in one particular week will not necessarily be reflected in that week's performance figures. This can easily lead to declining confidence and motivation. The PAS gives you the opportunity of being rewarded now for the good work that you do (by knowing that you are progressing), and recognises the 'goodwill' value of every contact made. Over a period of time, you will accumulate statistical information such as the average number of calls per deal done. This means that every call you make has a clear value. Your task then is not only to make more calls but to make the calls more effective.

The PAS scheme focuses on ten different areas of success in a sales call from which you award yourself points. It is as simple as that. Week to week you coach yourself to ever-increasing performance levels against your previous achievements. You will also find that you manage your time better. Each day there will be a simple record form to complete as you go, which can also be used to remind you of call-backs, etc. At the end of each week, you study your performance and set your own achievement targets for the following week, which should be at least a 10% improvement.

Every Monday morning you can review your PAS forms to discuss results and what can be done to improve.

PAS Daily Activity Sheet

One point awarded for each of the following:

1. Your company name plugged.
2. Relevant contact name(s) established.
3. Rapport established with relevant contact.
4. Favourable impression left.
5. Information on potential business.
6. Information on the company itself.
7. Objection overcome.
8. Client visit secured.
9. An order.
10. A sale (1 point per £100).

F – If you find yourself reticent to call strangers

Some people have a reticence to talk to strangers about what their business offers. Whatever you do, never take rejection personally – instead value it as feedback. Taking it personally can lead to a fear of rejection and produce call reluctance. As an entrepreneur, unlike employees, there is no one to kick your butt into action. You have to do it yourself and it is too easy to think of excuses. It is a reticence that is easily overcome. If it does not concern you, skip this section.

It could be that somewhere in your mind you have the belief that what you are offering is in question. This could lead to a feeling of manipulating someone for personal gain. If this is the case, your lack of belief will hold you back. You need to find out exactly what is troubling you and address it. What are your thoughts just before making that call or contact?

If you are generally a bit nervous, you probably just need a confidence boost. If it is something you are doing for the first time, all you need to do is makes six calls. The first level of confidence at anything is familiarity. From then on you will be familiar with what to say and how to react to the responses. If this is not enough, here are two more simple techniques – make telephone calls standing up and look down whilst you are making the call.

For these techniques to work, it is not necessary to understand why. For the curious, it is because before we make or receive a telephone call, we make a mental picture in our mind of the person at the other end. When that picture is at a level higher than ourselves, most of us find it intimidating. If it is lower, we feel confident. In training seminars, I get people to talk to each other once from standing on a chair and once from sitting on the floor. The recipient usually reports a dramatically different experience from each exercise. Try it with someone and you will be surprised.

In a later chapter we will be looking at specific telephone techniques, which will increase your confidence and improve the quality of each call you make.

G – Getting to and keeping at ten

Our productivity and success rate is mostly determined by our level of enthusiasm, energy, positive attitude and motivation. Let us say that our highest level of motivation and productivity is ten and the lowest zero. Therefore we all should want to consistently maintain a ten level irrespective of what the 'world' throws at us. If we are leading a team, our level will strongly influence them. It will also positively influence customers. We should therefore also help others to keep at ten.

The following pointers will help you.

- Remember that success is a decision.
- You need a 'why' more than a 'how' to get what you want.
- You must have a real passion for what you want.
- If you operate below 10, you are cutting profits.
- Being at 10 is determined by what you focus on.
- Your focus is determined by questions.
- Your body language determines your level as well as shows it.
- Positive words help get and keep you at 10.
- Negative (moving away from) motivation is more powerful.
- Write a list of your favourite positive words and keep them near you.
- Use of negative words gets you down from 10.
- Ban the use of negative words.
- Positive tone of voice helps get you and keep you at 10.
- What you picture and hear internally determines how you feel.
- Help others to get and keep at 10 and they will help you.
- Whatever level you are at you will draw those around you to your level.

Make the success decision to do whatever it takes to keep at a ten. Every word spoken or thought creates images and sounds in our mind. In turn, these trigger off feelings. That is why when someone asks me how I feel I usually say 'brilliant'. Some people say, 'not bad', which has two negative words in it! Avoid that response and feel the difference in your week. Here are some example positive words – incorporate them into your daily vocabulary, whilst making a point to delete negative ones.

Accomplishment	Achievement	Better
Best	Excellent	Fantastic
Good	Impressive	Perfect
Reward	Satisfaction	Superb
Success	Winner	Yes!

Progress now:

Write in 24 positive words below and make a decision to use them habitually.

You're half way through your goal, but can't quite make it to the end. What can you do? You can become a fortune teller. This is much easier than it sounds. You don't need any special powers, only your memory and your dreams.

The first step is to see into the past. Remember when you first created your goal. Remember the desire and dedication you had. Remember the main reasons you started in the first place. If you decided to lose weight, what was the reason that sparked your goal decision?

Just thinking about why you started can get you going again. Repeating your first thoughts and words about your goal will serve as a boost to your confidence and motivation. As time goes on, we sometimes forget why we started something in the first place. It is very important to remember the why and not only the how. After you look into the past, it's time to look in the opposite direction.

The next step is to see into the future. Think about the end of your goal, the time you finally accomplish your task. Think about how great you'll feel, how happy you'll be, and how much better off you'll be. You have to see the picture in your mind. Close your eyes and put yourself weeks, months, or years into the future.

This can help to keep you focused on your goals. Having a clear picture of where you are going to be will keep you motivated during the time in between. Once you see into the past, and look to the future, you will find the motivation to keep going.

H – Always make one more call

At the end of the day when you are tired, don't stop but set yourself a small target to achieve first. Have you noticed on a day before you go on holiday how much more you can achieve? Well, I suggest you work every day like that. One more call made each day is five a week, 20 per month and the marginal productivity of this can be significant when the longer timescale is looked at.

In any election, one vote more than your opponent means you win everything. In athletics, one nose in front of your competitor means you win everything. That one more call more can have the same effect for you. Any action you take towards your goals gets you that little bit closer to it. Might not seem like a lot of difference at the time but every distance travelled is a summation of a lot of small distances!

What metaphor are you running now? If you record the last five minutes of when you spoke, or write down a couple of paragraphs on your current thoughts, your metaphors will drop out. For most men in business, I have found the two most common are sports and military. With women, I have found have more variety, housekeeping is common (done and dusted) and also gardening (watering flowers). Anyway, the one you are running is not the most important. It is the ones you are not running that are important. These are the ones that give you access to different perspectives, that leads to new ideas, answers and so on.

If your language keeps referring to gardening, this suggests that you see your business in the same way that you would see a garden. This can be advantageous in as much it will teach you that you have to have patience and persistence. Two excellent qualities for business. Results don't come quickly in a gardening, so you have to have a long-term perspective. Equally, often in business we need to do things quickly against competition. Someone who talks in terms of athletics would be more in tune with where they need to be. If you needed to get the most out of a team, someone who talks about rugby or another team sport might have a more appropriate metaphor, a way of thinking.

Most people stick to one or two for 90% of the time. I would suggest that you deliberately have one to fit every occasion.

Progress now:

Complete the following list:

Metaphor	Appropriate Use
1. Gardening	Patience and persistence
2. Sprinting	Competitiveness and urgency
3. Football	Team building, leadership
4.	
5.	
6.	
7.	
8.	
9.	
10.	

When you go into a McDonald's, do you tend to sit in much the same place – nearest available seat, upstairs, against the wall? When you go to the cinema, do you sit in much the same seat? It is all about breaking habits and replacing them with more appropriate ones.

I – Public speaking

Often entrepreneurs are called upon to make presentations to large audiences. Large for this purpose could mean anything above two people. Most entrepreneurs who are not making presentations of this nature should be. These can be talks at the local chamber of commerce, associations, conferences, customer seminars and so on. Often you may have to present to a multiple audience at a client's establishment. How to prepare what you are going to say, using PowerPoint and other equipment is well covered in available literature and people are generally confident in this area. I get a lot of callers though asking me to help them with their fears, even phobias, related to public speaking. For this reason I consider it appropriate to include it here.

There are two elements to building confidence to offer public speaking. The first is becoming familiar with basic public speaking techniques. This in itself boosts confidence whilst improving the quality and control of the presentation.

The first technique I will tell you is called the 'yes set'. All you have to do is make three statements to which the entire audience mentally and physically nods and says yes. This establishes a group rapport and will have them accepting your following statements a lot more easily. People start to develop habits after three repetitions. For example:

Hello everybody, my name is Alex McMillan. *(yes he is)*
We are here to day to learn some new techniques on selling for entrepreneurs. *(yes we are)*
Despite the fact it is raining and cold outside… *(yes it is)*
… we are going to have a warm and fun learning experience. *(yes we are)*

Progress now:

Prepare some simple opening statements in line with the above formula for your next presentation.

The second technique I call 'Positive Universals'. It is a simple technique that builds on the 'yes set' and guarantees you rapport and gains it back at any time that you feel it might be waning. All you have to do is ask the audience questions where you know the answer will be the same for everyone. This has the effect of suggesting that audience members have something in common, however slight the level. You can make the technique more powerful and useful to you by incorporating in it positive experiences. For example:

'Can everyone here think of something that they would really love to have for Christmas?'

Not only is everyone now in rapport, you have also led their mental focus on to positive, happy ground.

Progress now:

Think of three examples of the above technique that you could use.

My third technique is what I call 'Outside In'. Most inexperienced presenters have their focus is on the inside, which they then transmit out. The more professional and successful approach is by doing the opposite. Your focus has to be outside of your head and on the audience all the time. Watch and listen to them and react accordingly. If they look bored, change your tack – if they look confused, explain it again etc, etc, etc. A good presentation is defined by how *they* thought it went, not how you thought it went. Have a clear structure for your talk prepared. When you start, trust me, if you know what you're talking about, the words will be there for you, and your unconscious will sort them into order all by itself.

For more tips on motivation, read *'Motivator'* by Frances Coombes – the best book I have ever read on the subject.

7

Questions Worth Asking

'Will you look back on life and say, 'I wish I had' or 'I'm glad I did'?'
Zig Ziglar

*'Even if you are on the right track,
you'll get run over if you just sit there.'*
Will Rogers

*'I'm sick and tired of hearing things from uptight, short-sighted,
narrow-minded hypocrites.
All I want is the truth – just give me some truth.'*
John Lennon

This chapter ...

A   Questioning techniques
B   Selling is simple
C   What can questions achieve?
D   Our own perception of the world
E   Barrier breakers
F   Bridge builders
G   Confusion clearers
H   There is always an easier way!

A – Questioning techniques

A co-founder of NLP, John Grinder, a Professor of Linguistics at the University of California, modelled America's greatest communicators. This included Dr Milton Erickson, who had revolutionised what had been traditional hypnosis and who was President of the American Society for Hypnosis and Hypnotherapy. As a professor of linguistics, observing the effects of Erickson's language patterns on his patients amazed him. These successful patterns that were teased out appear in two volumes in the bibliography. Interestingly, it was later established from modelling top performing sales superstars that, unknowingly, these patterns were getting them their exceptional results in their communication.

From this and other NLP research, there are two fundamental NLP models of language: the Meta model, which is a set of questions that gets straight to the core issues, and the Milton model, which gains access to the unconscious mind. There is nothing I have experienced in linguistic communication as powerful and appropriate to selling as these two models. The questioning techniques in this chapter have been developed from these original ideas to be of practical use in building a business.

To learn how to take advantage of these language patterns is like learning to drive a car. You do not need to understand why or how they work to be totally competent using them. You do, however, need someone who can teach you these skills without using jargon, thus making them practical and of immediate effect to a business person. Then a little practice and feedback from your own experience of applying them will lead to a rapidly growing confidence, refinement and habitual use.

Let us look at how people selling often dig themselves into a hole with the wrong question.

Sales person: Would you like to give me an order then?
Future Client: Thanks for calling but I'll leave it for now.
Sales person: Can I ask why that is?
Future Client: Because...

Most sales people regularly ask 'why' questions, particularly when up against a rejection. This produces in the prospect a virtually automatic response beginning with 'because'. That in turn produces all the reasons why not to buy. And while the future client is speaking, his mental state has gone into 'I do not want to buy' mode, and continually searches for more and more reasons for his decision. This has the effect of making him even more convinced that it was a right decision. Then the salesperson produces the 'buts' and starts stressing benefits, sounding more and more desperate as the sale becomes harder and harder to retrieve.

Instead, try opening the customer's mind. Better still, expand it by concentrating on owning your products or enjoying your services. Replace why questions with:

> "What positive benefits do you think could happen if you did buy from us?'
> 'What is the one thing you need to know in order to be interested?'
> 'What exactly can I do for you'?
> "What would I have to do to win your business?'

These questions will get you out of the ping-pong 'he says, you say' mentality and lead the conversation somewhere fruitful. Try it and see what happens. They may well lead to objections, which is good, as in order to manage objections, you first need to establish what they are. From that information you can determine the right key that will let the customer in.

B – Selling Is simple

I know an entrepreneur who set up her own office products company. At the final stage of the recruitment process, she would send her candidates to a known 'tough' customer. If they succeeded and got an order, they got the job. Recently they were recruiting and I enquired about the progress of the candidates.

The first one tried the 'nice guy, I am your friend' approach. He introduced himself, talked around the subject to get the prospect relaxed. When he had accomplished this he asked lots of questions in a very soft way, questions that led the prospect to answers requiring the use of his products as the solution. He was surprised therefore, when he gave a closing question, that the prospect said: 'Thanks for coming – I will bear you in mind when I am next ordering.' He had made the mistake of asking a question beginning 'Why ...'. This was, of course, responded to with an answer starting 'Because ...', and all the resistance came out.

The second salesperson had a different approach. He believed all a customer was really interested in was the best possible price. He said 'hello' and went into a presentation emphasising that his quality products were the most competitively priced and that he guaranteed that he would beat any competitor. His closing question was equally straightforward: 'So, what do you say?' He got an even more straightforward answer: 'No'. He then went through again what were to him the unbeatable benefits to the prospect. Alas, to no avail. He left bemused and baffled, believing that a competitor had already got better prices somewhere else.

The third sales representative was a lady who had built a reputation for winning in very difficult situations. She introduced herself and very professionally asked a series of questions eliciting a lot of useful information. She finished with what is known as the alternative close, 'Would you prefer delivery on Mondays or Fridays?' The prospect used to teach English and immediately recognised the presupposition as a selling technique. He replied: 'Would you prefer I turn you down now or at the end of the week?' He'd clearly got her. If she had laughed and admitted her attempt to close, she would still have stood a chance. However, she 'lost her cool' and made fumbled attempts to cover her tactics. 'Sorry, what do you mean … I was just asking … to find out.' She was not convincing.

The fourth sales representative, knowing of the previous candidates' failure, went up to the prospect and said: 'I know that many sales people have tried to get your business and failed. Can I ask you just one simple question?' 'Yes, go ahead.' 'What would I have to do in order to win your business?' The prospect told him. 'Not try to use any fancy closing techniques to trap me into buying. All I want to see is your products, your prices and to be convinced that I will receive good, honest service.' The representative said: 'Here is a sample of a product. They are £25 each and I will do whatever it takes within my power to keep you as a satisfied customer.' He got the order.

The one right question will have the effect of a cruise missile. Straight to the target with the desired result.

Unseen by the successful representative, an observer had been watching the discourse and had noticed some absolutely amazing things about the two people's body language, postures, tones of voice, words, linguistic patterns and even breathing. He went up to the representative and asked him if he had done this deliberately or by intuition. More on that in the next chapter.

C – What can questions achieve?

Before you read further, write down twelve potential benefits arising from asking the right questions in a sales situation.

1.

2.

3.

4.

5.

6.

7.

8.

9.

10.

11.

12.

The following is a list of answers produced by a cross-sectional group from a recent seminar. How do they compare to your answers?

Establishing facts
Qualifying potential customers
Establishing requirements
Establishing individual needs
Identifying decision-makers
Identifying decision influencers
Discovering personality type of future client
Establishing size of budget
Establishing price constraints
Establishing the target's position with regard to competitors
Revealing motivation ('hot buttons')
Establishing relationships
Determining whether one-off or ongoing customer potential
Discovering external relationships
Helping to create rapport
Opportunities for listening and observing
Enabling understanding and clarification

Test closing
Closing
Opening
Communicating embedded commands
Tag questions*
Changing customer's 'state of mind'
Establishing presuppositions.

*A tag question makes a statement and then ties your agreement in. Adding a tag question to the end of a statement makes it stronger in the listener's mind. For example:

The products are good, aren't they?
We all like good value, don't we?
Value For Money is important, isn't it?
Speed of delivery is an important issue, isn't it?
The products meet the specification, don't they?

They are best used when reflecting back something that the prospect has said. He cannot therefore disagree and you are creating a run of affirmatives.

Your main task in a sales presentation is to find out how you can help the future client. This you do with questioning – but not any old questions. They have to direct the prospect's mind to where you want to get to, eliciting information and then using this information to open the client's mind to new choices. The real talent, once you have an armoury of precision questions, is to know what questions to ask and clear the fog, the red herrings and so on, along the way. This is best done by having a clear outcome in mind before you start. You have to find out what is happening in their mind, not yours. To them this is reality, irrespective of any evidence to the contrary. Don't fall into the trap of making assumptions; instead, use the homing questions that I am going to teach you. Your challenge is to elicit clarity through questions and then to make an offer in the client's own language in their own reality.

For example, questions to elicit the real needs of a future client should be something like the following. Notice that they have in built checks that they are the core needs.

For what purpose?
What will that do for you?
What will that allow you to do?
What do you want from a ...?

What are you looking for in a ...?
How will you know when you have ...?
What's important to you about ...?
What do you value most in a ...?

D – Our own perception of the world

The words that we all use during a conversation are not the experiences themselves. They are just the best verbal representation we can come up with. This is worth bearing in mind the next time that you have put a question to a prospect and are listening to his response. How precise is he?

The principal aim of your sales presentation is to elicit information to enable you to offer a deal that will be accepted by your prospect. If you don't get the right information, your persuasive efforts will miss their mark and leave you without the sale. The questioning techniques taught in this book will give you the linguistic technology to home in on the specific information necessary to close a deal. Have you ever been confident of winning an account only to be surprised to learn that it went to the competition? That is because your questioning wasn't precise enough to uncover the buyer's strategies, motivation and needs. Or your understanding of the words he was using had a different meaning in his mind than it did in yours. Someone did it better.

For example, in the future customer's mind, 'I don't want to buy from this salesperson, because the last time that I bought this sort of product, the quality was poor. This led to the production line being stopped meaning thousands of pounds worth of product were written off. When I contacted the then sales rep, he didn't want to know. From now on I'll be wary of an attractive looking price and have 'quality' and 'after sales service' as my top priorities.'

Future customer: 'Good morning, what have you got to offer me?'

Sales Rep: 'Good morning, a great product range at prices that beat all of our competitors. How does that sound?'

The sales rep continues, totally missing the mark. The challenge to the salesperson is to uncover the first paragraph from the sentence that he receives. So the first step is to ask intelligent and precise questions with a clear outcome in mind (you are not there just to make friends).

Bear in mind that the value of a well chosen question is lost if you do not listen attentively to the response. In this context, remember that listening also means attention to tonality and careful observation of the speaker.

There are three types of homing-in or targeting questions – barrier breakers, bridge builders and confusion clearers.

E – Barrier breakers

Absolute barriers come in two main forms which I will refer to as 'brick walls' and 'sweeping statements', as further explained below.

Brick Walls

Examples of 'brick walls' are:

I can't give you the order.
I can't change suppliers at this time.
I won't consider using you again.

The targeting questions to deal with these must challenge assumptions about the past or habitual buying behaviour and introduce new options in the prospect's mind:

What would happen if you did?
How do you stop yourself from...?

Sweeping Statements

Examples of sweeping statements are:

I have never been satisfied buying insurance.
All salesmen in my experience tell lies.
Every purchase I make is through Bloggs & Co.
I always buy on the basis of lowest price.

When a future client makes such a statement, it is very rare for it to be true in the client's mind for all occasions. By getting them to show you the exception, you can prise it open, offering choices to the client that were not there before.

Targeting questions to deal with these would be along the following lines:

Never? All? Every? Always? Has there ever been a time when ...?

Bear in mind that a statement that the prospect makes will often provide choices as to what may be challenged. The real talent is deciding which question asked is most likely to lead the prospect to the desired outcome.

F – Bridge builders

Sometimes customer resistance is expressed in language that can be turned to your advantage, enabling you to pick on a point of expression and build a 'bridge' to cross the divide the customer is creating, and progress the dialogue. Examples are set out below:

Vague nouns and verbs

Statement: 'I want a better deal?'
Targeting question: 'What deal exactly would you like?'

Statement: 'He ripped me off.'
Targeting question: 'How exactly did he rip you off?'

Nouns made out of verbs

A verb is alive, dynamic, open to change. A noun is fixed, rigid, lifeless, unchangeable. We can therefore put life back in by changing the noun back to a verb. For example:

Statement: 'I have made my decision.'
Targeting question: 'How exactly did you decide?'

Missing people

Sometimes customers will make statements indicating that a third party has an influence on the decision. For example:

Statement: '   We'll think about this and come back to you.'
Targeting question: 'That's great, may I just ask who 'we' are exactly?'

Missing Information

Statements: 'I am not convinced.'   'I am undecided. '
Targeting questions: 'About what?' 'About whom?'

Missing Comparisons

Customers may make use of comparatives or superlatives with no mention of who you are being compared with.

Statement: 'Bloggs' products are better. '
Targeting question: 'Better, in what way?'
Statement: 'Bloggs' products are best.' Or,'Your product is too expensive.'
Targeting question: 'In comparison to what or whose?'

G – Confusion clearers

Sometimes the customer will make a statement which is confused, or makes unwarranted assumptions.

Tied statements

This is where two statements are ostensibly linked but the link between them has not been established and needs challenging.

Statement: 'I cannot decide today because my Purchasing Manager is out.'
Targeting question: 'How does his being out stop you from making a decision?'

Opinionated statements

This is the case where opinions, values and judgements are given without any supporting evidence. The source of the value needs to be recovered.

Statement: 'You will say anything to get the order. '
Targeting question: 'I am curious to know what leads you to believe that?'

Mind readers

Sometimes customers will indicate they know another person's thoughts on a matter.

Statement: 'My MD wouldn't like me to change suppliers. '
Targeting questions: 'How do you know that?' Or, 'What leads you to believe that?'

Cause and effect

Statement: 'Because of current policy I am restricted in my options.'
Targeting question: 'How specifically does current policy restrict you?'

Presuppositions

Sometimes a customer will make a statement including an incorrect presumption, or presupposition.

Statement: 'I cannot make a decision until I have your discount rates.'
Targeting question: 'What leads you to believe I have discount rates?'

Note that as well as challenging presuppositions in others, you too can use presuppositions or presumptions for your own purposes. They are persuasive because they make linguistic short cuts in the future client's mind. Consider the following:

Did you know that ...?
Are you aware that ...?
Perhaps you have already heard that ...?
Have you ever noticed the fact that ...?
Would it be fair to say that ...?
Would you agree with me that ...?
Would you agree with the experts that ...?

Difficult not to answer 'yes' to questions beginning with these words. Consider that you have not even heard the content yet and you are already agreeing. So will your future client. They are presuppositions because what follows is already established as fact.

This technique is even more powerful if you incorporate something the future client has already told you:

'Since you have already met the representatives from my competitors, would it be fair to say that if I can come up with a product that totally satisfies your needs at a competitive price, you could make a decision today?'

The 'alternative close' also involves a presupposition:

'Would you prefer this model in red or blue?'

This presupposes that you are going to buy.

Consider the following questions. Can you identify the presuppositions?

How easily can you make a choice today?
Are you still interested in a new car?
When would you like to begin to consider the alternatives?
Have you allocated your budget yet?
How many of the beneficial points that you have learned today do you
    plan on sharing with your staff this week?
Have you noticed how well this car matches your personality?
What would it take for you to make a decision today?

Progress now:

Think of three presuppositions that you could use in your sales presentation:

1.

2.

3.

Remember, the effect of a presupposition depends on the level of rapport. If you do not have rapport, the question might not be answered at all. It is only necessary that the prospect thinks of an answer even at a subconscious level for it to have its effect.

H – There is always an easier way!

Some students were having a charity race. The participants had to get to Aberdeen from Oxford without any money and without using public transport. For everybody who achieved it within 12 hours, £200 was donated to charity, within 24 hours, £100 and within the weekend, £25.

The different approaches to this problem by various students were incredible. Out of 145 entrants, only five completed the task winning the £200 for charity. Their approaches varied. One student chose to hitchhike. Nothing original in that – however, he was a mathematics student and he contacted the RAC and gained detailed information on traffic flows. Armed with this knowledge, he did not hitch in the same way as he would have driven. Those who went as they would have driven, were delayed by traffic congestion and they failed to meet the deadline. Another student contacted a car factory in Cowley and offered to deliver a car to Scotland free of charge. They were very pleased! At the end of the weekend, the students' union had calls from all over Britain, one even from Wales. How did he get there? The losers had lots of good reasons why they were disadvantaged or unlucky. The winners didn't think of it as much of an achievement. It was easy for them.

Now, let us see how we can get to our objective by the shortest route, by looking at two examples.

Future client:	'Your product is too expensive.'
Sales person:	'Compared to what?'
Future client:	'Well, compared to our present supplier, brand X.'
Sales person:	'How exactly does that product compare to mine?'
Future client:	'I don't know exactly.'
Sales person:	'That's interesting. What would you do if you were convinced that our product was of higher quality.'
Future client:	'I'd consider it, I guess if you proved that it was better quality.'
Sales person:	'What exactly could I do that would satisfy you beyond doubt that my product is of better quality?'
Future client:	'Well, if we used them in our factory, under our working conditions and the defective rate was significantly improved.'
Sales person:	'What exactly would that be worth to you?'

We have steered the conversation from generalisations to specifics. Now we are in a position to offer our solutions that meet the client's true needs, not just the apparent needs, in this case a lower price.

There is always a question you can ask that will lead you to the business. The second example is an ordering problem:

Future client:	'I have had a problem in the past when ordering new components.'
Sales person:	'A problem in ordering what specifically?'
Future client:	'Well, it's just that the quality has not always been what it could.'
Sales person:	'How exactly has the quality been lacking?'
Future client:	'You know, early failure of parts, defective units, that kind of thing.'
Sales person:	'Which parts in particular?'
Future client:	'Well now that you mention it, it seems to always be the control dials that are faulty.'
Sales person:	'What control dials are you using?'
Future client:	'The Science Partnership RX400 series mainly.'
Sales person:	'On what applications do you use the RX400?'
Future client:	'On radios.'
Sales person:	'On all of the radios?'

Future client:	'No, not really on all.'
Sales person:	'On which ones then?'
Future client:	'On the class A and B radios.'
Sales person:	'Let me touch base. Your main problem at the moment is to do with the control knobs on the Class A and B radios. Otherwise there are no major areas for concern at the moment?'
Future client:	'Yes, that's right.'
Sales person:	'OK. What would it be worth to your company to have a reliable source of control knobs for these classes of radio?'
Future client:	'Well, I suppose if they were reliable we would have less stoppages, which is our hidden cost. However we have used other suppliers before and never had the reliability we wanted.'
Sales person:	'Has there ever been a time of smooth production flow using these components?'
Future client:	'Well, now that you mention it, before our present supplier was taken over, quality was better. But we were paying higher prices then.'
Sales person:	'How does the previous higher price compare with the current additional price of stoppages?'
Future client:	'Mmm. I see your point.'
Sales person:	'OK. Let me tell you what I propose, and see what you think. My company's market research department has reported a lot of dissatisfaction from purchasers like yourself. The current market has made us all cost and price conscious in order to be competitive. In order to keep prices competitive, many companies have had to reduce their costs, which means that standards of quality have had to be compromised. The result is while some products appear cheaper in the short run, they can be considerably higher in the long run. Recognising this trend, our company's policy has been the opposite to our competitors. We have invested in R & D instead of cutting it and employed rigorous quality control standards in our factories. We believe, looked at over the long run, our products are the best value for money on the market. Can I suggest that you try us out in order to see for yourself?'
Future client:	'Yes, Okay.'

Sales person: 'What evidence would you need to know beyond reasonable doubt that our products were more suitable for your needs?'

Progress now:

Respond to these statements with a targeting question.

1. The competition has a better product.

 ⊕

2. If I get an attractive offer, I'll probably take it.

 ⊕

3. I can't do that at the moment.

 ⊕

4. I can't make a decision over the phone.

 ⊕

5. I never buy anything before thinking it over.

 ⊕

6. All you entrepreneur types promise the earth, but don't deliver.

 ⊕

7. I am looking for something different.

 ⊕

Progress now:

Write your own empowering versions of these 'self ask' questions.

1. How can I take total control of my sales results?

2. What is the most valuable question I can ask? *(To yourself prior to a sales presentation)*

3. What would I have to do in order to win your business? *(During a tough presentation when you are coming up against resistance. Notice the hidden presupposition.)*

4. How can I win this account?

5. What could I change in order to win your business?

6. What can I do today to excel?

7. How can I turn the situation to my advantage?

With the knowledge of what you have learnt, what new closing questions can you think of that are relevant for your business?

Before your next call, take a few moments to consider exactly what you hope to learn and accomplish. Then, based on the customer and situation, prepare a series of questions designed to elicit the responses you seek. Try them out in advance on colleagues and friends. You might be surprised at the reaction to what you thought was the 'perfect' question.

As a final tip, always pre-think your questions for phone work, have them printed and in front of you for quick reference. For example, when trying to get through secretaries, 'Would you put me through to Mr Smith, please?' is stronger than 'Is Mr Smith available?'.

8

How to Establish Rapport
Face to Face

'All the people that like us are we, and everyone else is they.'
Rudyard Kipling

'We may have all come on different ships,
but we are in the same boat now.'
Martin Luther King

This chapter ...

A Can rapport be developed with body language?
B What can you do to create rapport?
C Analysis of influence
D Posture pacing
E Establishing face-to-face rapport
F Matching breathing
G How do you know when you are in rapport?
H A practical illustration
I Assessing individual body talk

A – Can rapport be developed with body language?

In selling, there are two aspects of body language to consider. Reading the signals from the other person, and using your own body language to help produce sales. Most books focus on the first. If you are observant, most of the body language signals are obvious – it is no great secret. If you are passionate, enthusiastic and honest about what you offer, this will come across automatically through your body language. Rapport on the other hand means more abut reacting to where they are. Let us define exactly what rapport is, so we can see why it is so essential to establish as a key priority at the start of a communication. Rapport is:

- having something in common
- a state between two or more people that precedes influence
- sharing a 'personal chemistry' with your customer
- co-operative relationship
- being on the same wavelength as your customer
- being in tune with each other
- seeing things the same way
- when two act as one
- a like-mindedness.

Rapport is the ability to enter someone else's world so that they feel that you understand them, that you have a strong common bond. It is the ability to go fully from *your* perception of the world to *theirs*. When this sympathetic relationship or understanding is established, then an environment of trust, confidence and participation is developed. It will also make it easy for you to see things from their perspective, what good selling is all about.

B – What can you do to create rapport?

Have something in common – it is as simple as that. This requires a flexible attitude to leave your world and enter somebody else's to create rapport. The biggest barrier is thinking that other people look at the world in the same way you do. I have extensive experience with entrepreneurs in both increasing sales and motivating staff. The most common mistake is assuming other people are motivated the same way they are. Some of the questions I ask a new client include: *'What motivates your key customers?'* *'What motivates you?* and *'What motivates any staff you have?'* Few have clear answers, and yet these answers are absolutely crucial to massively increasing the size and profits of their business. There is no right way to view the world, hence the saying, 'The customer is always right'. If you wish to change their view, you first have to establish rapport with them, otherwise you will be talking to a brick wall!

If you are flexible, you can develop rapport with everybody. If you find yourself up against what appears to be resistance, this is your signal to be flexible and try a different tack. Before the end of this chapter, you will have gone a long way towards mastering these skills. At this point your mastery will only be developed by 'going live', practising your skills and observing the results you attain. This will lead to new and better habits being formed. At this point, you will find it difficult not to develop near instant rapport with everyone you meet. I always say to people on my sales business development trainings, that learning and understanding techniques won't improve your results, new habits will.

When people are in rapport, they match each other's behaviour at various levels and the opposite is also true. When people are not in rapport, they mismatch at various levels. Some of these levels are more significant than others; this is discussed in the next chapter.

Mastering the skill of building rapport requires the ability to be sensitive and observant to information given by the client. Then to use this information by taking action, being flexible and adjusting your response accordingly. Once you have been taught the techniques, mastery depends on your ability to perceive other people's postures, gestures and speech patterns and then the elegance in which you can match them.

When people think similar they look similar.

When people look similar they think similar.

Progress now:

What can you do to develop rapport on a client visit?

C – Analysis of influence

I have previously referred to the relative influence of the three ways in which we communicate. This shows that establishing a good rapport with body language will be far easier than achieving it with words. Most of us, however, rely on words to develop this common bond and are more adept at it, despite the fact that developing a common bond with body talk is so simple and so powerful. One test concluded that the relative influences were 55% via body language, 38% tonality and only 7% words. For theorists, those figures and the research can be looked at more deeply. For our practical purpose, this is enough information. It means that, if true, the difference in influences between the written word and something said face-to-face can be represented as follows:

Good morning Alex, how are you today?

| **Written** | ➔ | **words** | ⬅ |
| **Face-to-face** | ➔ body language ⬌ tonality ⬌ words ⬅ |

Progress now:

> What changes will you make personally in light of the above knowledge?

D – Posture pacing

As you now know, there is much more for the receiver to perceive from a given communication than the communicator can know consciously. The notion that there are large portions of our communicated behaviour unavailable to ourselves, yet revealed to the world, can be disconcerting. However carefully we might choose our words, the rest of our behaviour speaks most eloquently to the knowledgeable receiver.

Mirroring is not the same as mimicry. Mimicry is exaggeration of a behavioural feature. Mirroring is the subtle, behavioural reflection of the meaningful, unconscious communications each of us offers to the attentive receiver. At first, mirroring can sometimes feel awkward, even manipulative.

It soon becomes unconscious and respectful. It is only necessary to become *similar* in practice, not exactly the same.

The level of rapport you establish with someone is determined by your ability to pace them. Pacing means getting in rhythm with that person. If you are by nature a good listener and flexible you will do all the right things anyway. You communicate with someone through body language the second you meet them. You cannot not influence them even if you remain quiet, and it only takes a matter of seconds to establish rapport.

Modern psychology has now firmly established that conscious or unconscious pacing, i.e. matching of patterns, is what determines the state of rapport. Most sales people who call on me don't do this – instead they operate in their own patterns of behaviour. When they do develop rapport, it is by accident.

When you match body language as well as developing rapport, something else of value happens. As our brain and body are part of one system, by matching you will also be accessing the same parts of your brain as they are. This will give you some surprisingly accurate intuitive thoughts as to what they are thinking, what they will do next and how they may react to any proposal. Even better news, this will come to you unconsciously – no effort other than the 'matching' is required. So go with your instincts: these are based on a lot more reasoning than you realise and will usually be correct. Like a lot of things in this book, you may find this hard to believe without the evidence of personal experience. So, please experiment and see what you find.

E – Establishing face-to-face rapport

We know that 55% of communication is by body talk. So where do you think the greatest potential is for establishing rapport? Face-to-face rapport is most effectively achieved by simply adopting a similar body language to theirs. The main areas of matching body language can be summarised as follows:

- similar movements
- posture
- orientation
- weight distribution
- gestures (arms, hands, legs, and feet)
- facial expression

- eye contact
- rate of blinking
- breathing
- head tilting
- eye squinting
- flicks of the eyebrows.

When you use the technique of matching, your clients will have the subjective experience of being really understood. After all, you are speaking their body language. You cannot verbally talk your way out of problems you body talk yourself into. You can, however, behave your way out of problems you talk yourself into.

After a short period of time as a people watcher, you will notice that people instinctively mirror each other as they develop rapport. You can now begin to do so deliberately to achieve specific outcomes. Start by mirroring just one aspect of another person's behaviour while talking to them. When this is easy and becomes second nature, add another, match things such as arm movements while talking, until you are mirroring without thinking about it.

The more you practise, the more you will become aware of the rhythms that you and others generate. Notice the degree to which couples mis-match at every level when they fall out, in contrast to when they are doing well with one another.

Beware of attaching 'labels' to body language. Different body posture changes can mean different things for different people. You must first get into their world and then you will realise what a particular body posture means for them. Remember that the brain and body are parts of a holistic system. Neurology and physiology are directly related. In other words, when you move in unison with someone you are accessing the same parts of your brain as they are theirs, which is why rapport is created. More than rapport, and as you become successful at making the distinctions, you will almost always know more about your prospect's continuing experience than the prospects themselves are consciously aware of.

Progress now:

Next time you are out, observe people and see what you notice with reference to the above.

F – Matching breathing

Many people find the concept of matching breathing to establish rapport strange, when they first learn of it. Consider this: the human body requires the supply of three key resources in order to maintain life – food, water and air. If you fast and deny yourself food, you will probably last for between three to six months. If you fast by cutting out water you will probably live for three to six days. If you are denied breath you are unlikely to live as long as six to eight minutes. The point is that air is the most crucial thing to the body, not food and water. Eastern mystics have always been aware of this and any book on Yoga will teach you a range of breathing exercises that will better utilise this resource in the body.

Our breathing rate is part of the same system life force as our pulse, blinking and a whole range of bodily processes. By matching breathing, you are immediately setting up what is known technically as a biofeedback loop and locking straight in to somebody's internal world. I like to explain it in terms of tuning in to their frequency.

Calibrating a person's breathing becomes easier with practice and training. It is easier to notice than you might think, it is just a matter of focus. Some people breathe so strongly it is quite clear; in others you can detect a slight movement up and down of their shoulders relative to a fixed point behind. Some people sigh frequently, which gives the pattern. People are, of course, breathing out while they are talking. If you want to develop your skill at this technique get two friends to help you. Have one of them stand behind the other who is sitting. Standing behind is a good point to observe breathing. Have this person do nothing other than observe the breathing of the seated person from close quarters – then to show it to you by raising their hand up and down with large sweeps in time and size with the breathing. Observing this you can pace the hand movements easily and talk in the same patterns. Practise at least a dozen times like this in half-hour sessions and you will start to find that it is becoming habitual. Taking away the support then will not make any difference as you have trained your sensory antennae to a new level.

As mentioned earlier, be careful of interpreting body language that basically says 'x posture means y' apart from the most obvious. You may interpret somebody sighing as being bored or frustrated, whereas actually they have mild asthma. This does not tell you how to utilise this knowledge with reference to your objectives. If somebody's fist is banging on the desk, it is probably a fair guess that they are angry. However, when we are trying to interpret subtle postures or changes in posture you can make sweeping generalisations but they are not going to be true for everybody. By pacing you can calibrate for the individual. In other words, when Harry folds his arms it means that he is resistant. When Mary folds her arms it means that she is cold. When John folds his arms it is because he is conscious of his paunch and wishes to cover it. By pacing, we are avoiding the risk of being wrong and we respect everybody as an individual.

Have you ever observed total strangers at a football match? As the game progresses they sway together, applaud, jump up, chant, cheer and boo together. The fans on both sides do everything in unison with their fellow fans and at different times to the opponent fans. They are establishing and developing a deeper rapport with each other whilst moving further away from the facing fans. Bad behaviour when the two conflicting groups meet is not so much surprising as inevitable!

G – How do you know when you are in rapport?

Simply, when you change your posture and the other party then mirrors you. Next time you are out, observe the postures people adopt in relation to who they are with or talking to. See if your own evidence supports the idea that when people are in rapport their posture is similar. Conversely, when people are not, are their postures clearly different? When in rapport, what do you find happens if one changes posture?

Watch people in a restaurant, a pub, wine bar or night club, perhaps a couple out together, or a sales representative entertaining a client. When they are in rapport do they tend to retain eye contact, nod simultaneously, heads moving in similar ways, shoulders at the same angle, arms in the same posture? It is essential that you go out and observe this for yourself. If you do, you will create a belief change and you will find your own patterns beginning to change automatically to gain rapport.

Posture pacing someone means first noticing how they use their body language. It may be a clap of the hands, a tap on the desk or drawing imaginary pictures in front of themselves. If you describe your points back to them, drawing them out in this way, it will be meaningful in the customer's world. It gets your message through in their language. Some may consider this manipulative – I consider it service. I think that it is the sales person's duty to talk the future client's language and develop rapport in any way possible. Have you ever entered a showroom and been ignored, and walked out? Then gone into another showroom, met a professional who developed rapport and got into your way of seeing the world? From this information he clearly explained to you the benefits of a particular product that suited you. He then closed the deal. That is what I want, in fact that is what most people want from a salesperson. I enjoy spending money and I want to buy things that are going to add value to my life. I consider it exploitative when this is not done and I just come up against pushiness, pressure, lack of integrity or just not being listened to.

I am not saying that you have to mirror every slight movement; it need not be so literal that it is obvious. Posture pacing is an unconscious mind communication. Unless we deliberately set out to do so, we do not consciously notice the body talk of others. Ask yourself what the postures were on the last three meetings that you had. I suspect that you had to really think about it. During a sales presentation, you have a lot to think about. Matching body language while thinking about what to say, handling objections and listening attentively is rather a lot to do. In fact your conscious mind can only process up to nine pieces of information at a time. Clearly a lot has to be filtered out and concentration has to be placed on the most critical parts. The way to do this is to develop your body language rapport skills to a level where it is carried out unconsciously. In other words, every time you meet someone, you automatically match them without realising you are doing it. That way your conscious mind is left free to pay attention and listen.

Progress now:

When you think you are in rapport with someone in a face-to-face meeting, move your arm and see if they follow.

H – A practical illustration

Once I accompanied a colleague on a sales presentation to pitch for an assignment to recruit a Financial Director for a major manufacturer of aircraft components in Surrey. My colleague took the lead and I supported him. Not having to concentrate on what I was going to say next I had the opportunity to concentrate on what I could observe.

I watched every movement and paced it. I moved forward, moved my arms and even matched his breathing. I then tried leading the client to a more relaxed posture by sitting back and slowing my breathing rate. The client followed. I started to smile increasingly. He followed. The first time this happens it can frankly be a bit spooky. Remember that the objective in sales is to understand somebody else, make the trouble to get into their world so that you can suggest a solution that meets their needs. Bear in mind that he never directly looked at me during the presentation, as he was concentrating on the dialogue he was having with my partner. We had established an empathy bond on a totally non-verbal level. The point is that non-verbal rapport is all that you need. When you have rapport, you do not have to keep agreeing with the client, you can disagree verbally and still maintain rapport and your differing views will be considered openly.

We got the deal by offering something that exactly met his needs, there and then, against stiff competition. That is one of the things I like about maintaining rapport through body language alone. You are not tempted to agree when you do not in fact agree and still know that you are not risking the deal.

The more you pace non-verbally, the more you will notice how different everybody's posture and movements are. Remember, by pacing their physiology you will also be accessing the same neurological circuits in your brain. This means that you will start receiving 'intuitions' about what he or she is going to do or say next. You will literally be getting into their world more and more. This is paying respect, and not forcing your 'model of the world' on them. Only when you have entered their world, will you know what is best for the future client. Establishing this, pointing it out and then supplying it is professional selling. Establishing it and realising that what you offer is not the best solution for the prospect and suggesting alternatives is professional selling. Pretending that your goods and services match his requirements when you do not believe it, is negative manipulation and unethical. No respectable company will do this. Few customers will supply references, referrals or future orders. Thinking long-term while working under extreme short-term pressures (targets/cash crisis) is one of the things that separates the very top performing sales people from the average.

When you have rapport, the next stage is to lead the prospect to where you want him to go. Now you go ahead changing their behaviour by getting them to follow your lead. You can test if you have rapport by changing your body language in some way, such as crossed-legged to uncrossed and seeing if they follow. They are now receptive to what you want to say and you can lead the conversation. You can proceed to find their needs and then match your products or services to them. Because you are in a heightened state of rapport, repetitive test closing will be unnecessary.

I – Assessing individual body talk

There are so many different possible expressions, combinations and permutations in body talk that a full listing would read like a Spanish-to-English dictionary (to someone who doesn't speak Spanish). In the face alone, with its complex system of muscles, there are over 15,000 different expressions that are possible. The more prominent ones are fairly obvious, and are certainly worth knowing. But what I am interested in here is the more subtle ones that are peculiar to the individual and are far more numerous. Body language signs are different for different people. Therefore you have to calibrate for each individual.

The best way to develop your skill in understanding body language is not by studying books at all. Get a partner to stand to the left of you, and then say something that he agrees with and believes passionately. Then get him to stand to the right of you, and say something that is an outright lie. Observe every muscle in his face; what was different? Colour, colour change, a slight twitch somewhere before a lie, a flick of the brow, a slower speed or different volume? Repeat the drill until you are confident that you have calibrated his physiological unconscious responses. Then get him to say something without telling you if it is truth or lie and see if you can guess which it is. If you can, you have learnt the art of personal body language calibration. He would have to have the acting ability of Dustin Hoffman to disguise his true feelings.

As you become more adept, you can repeat the exercise using less extreme examples. For example, get your partner to make statements about foods they like and foods they don't like. After each practice session you will be surprised at just how much information you can read from his or her face.

9

How To Establish Rapport
on the Telephone

'Give every man thy ear, but few thy voice.'
William Shakespeare

'You can make more friends in two months by becoming interested in other people than you can in two years by trying to get other people interested in you.'
Dale Carnegie

This chapter ...

A   **Rapport on the telephone**
B   **Listening in on a world of difference**
C   **High-level pacing**
D   **The hierarchy of rapport**
E   **Moving on once rapport is established**

A – Rapport on the telephone

I cannot imagine any entrepreneur who does not have to sell on the telephone. As a call travels a variety of distances instantaneously, it is perhaps the best and fastest way to sell. The biggest drawback is time spent finding out that the person you wanted is not in – however the advent of mobile telephones has reduced this considerably. On the telephone, you influence the other speaker with the words that you say and also the way (tonality) that you say them.

What percentage respectively, do words and tonality have on influencing the listener?

a) 75% words   25% tonality
b) 50% words   50% tonality
c) 25% words   75% tonality

One study concluded that 84% of the message on the telephone is communicated through how you speak (tonality) and only 16% through words.

'My quality of after-sales service is excellent.'
'Would you mind ... ...,'
'Could I ask you ... ...,'

Telephone: ➔   **Tonality**   ←➔ **Words** ←

The point being is that how you say the above will be what determines if the listener is convinced or not!

Progress now:

Try this exercise and have fun now with a partner.

1. Make a list of ten positive words and ten negative words.
2. First speak the positive words but with a negative tone to your partner.
3. Then speak the negative words but with a positive tone to your partner.
4. Ask which experience your partner found the most uplifting.

When I have done this in training situations, everyone has found that the most uplifting experience is when the negative words are used. Interestingly, most people found it difficult to use words that did not align with their body language.

Let us therefore look at tonality first. Like body language, rapport is developed by matching, so what can we match?

When matched, your tone of voice, i.e. your rhythm, speed, timbre, pitch, volume, enthusiasm and so on, will develop near instant rapport, irrespective of what is being said. Clearly what is being said can enhance or work against this 'tonal' rapport, but the effect is minimal. The unconscious mind, where the decisions are made, will pick up everything in your tone, although it may not communicate its knowledge to the conscious mind. That is why this is sometimes hard to believe. You are considering it consciously.

It follows that telephone selling based upon scripts could potentially be improved six times. There is a lot more to it than 'Smile as you dial'. In fact, that approach on many occasions will lose you sales. However NLP techniques can be learnt and applied by anyone, guaranteeing near instant rapport. When this happens, you will start to look forward to telephone canvassing and the constant 'buzz' of success that it brings them. After applying these techniques, you will find that you change excuses into results.

Taking the prospect's words, attaching *your* meaning to them, translating them into the language *you* use, and communicating from *your* linguistic style, are all steps that are arbitrary on your part, and are quite likely to lead to confusion.

Using the language of *your client* is the best way to have an impact on him or her. Words represent experience, and even though we use a common language, our experiences are necessarily different. If you use somebody's own words back to them, they will instinctively feel that they have been understood.

Imagine you are about to call someone. Unknown to you, they have had a whole month of bad news and to top it all their wife has just rung and said that the house is flooded from a burst water main. Having just finished a book called *'Smile As You Dial'*, you open: 'Hi, good morning, isn't it wonderful? Hey, you sound down, what's the matter? Cheer up, I'm sure everything is going to work out great.' All said with a lively enthusiastic tonality. Their reaction would be one of the following:

1. Totally uplifted by this completely positive person, the client will forget his problems and consider placing a big order … or
2. He will be totally wound up, and wonder why it is always him who has these problems, why it is him who always get these phone calls. Then he will tell you to get lost, politely if you are lucky.

I think you will agree it is answer two. You have to be sensitive and then responsive. Can I suggest that when on the phone (as opposed to face-to-face, when body talk will immediately indicate the mood of the prospect) you match everything you can, words and tone, remembering that getting the tone right will have a far greater effect than the words. However, practise one thing at a time. In your next ten calls, speak back to callers in the same tone of voice that they use, fast/slow, enthusiastic/calm, changing tempo/monotone, changing pitch/constant pitch, etc. If you are still not convinced, try mismatching some calls and see how much rapport develops.

In tonal matching, you can find yourself emotionally pacing. You call a person in a very bad mood. They say: 'Oh dear, I suppose you're looking for an order. We are totally overwhelmed here today.' You respond: 'Oh dear, what exactly is the problem?' in a similar tone of voice. You experience the emotion of the moment with them, whatever that emotion happens to be. Matching a strong emotion gets you strong rapport fast.

Now think about this. Think of a time recently in your life when you have found yourself with somebody who was emotional, positively or negatively. Remember how you reacted to them and what effect this had on them. If you are still not convinced, try mismatching and watch the result. The next time you are with someone who is angry, or 'throwing a wobbly', say 'calm down', or 'stop shouting', in a really calm voice. In my experience this throws oil on the fire. Next time say in a matching volume and style, **'Oh no, I can really understand why you are angry'** and then lead on to calmer grounds.

B – Listening in on a world of difference

Okay, so it's not what you say but how you say it. Have you noticed that people speak at different speeds? We speak at the rate which is comfortable for us. In fact, we change our speed due to changes in our internal state. However, we all have a 'default' rate that we are most comfortable with. If we are comfortable speaking at this rate, it follows that we would find it easier to listen to someone speaking at the same speed. Have you ever had the experience of listening to someone who talks very fast and finding it difficult to communicate with them? Or the opposite, somebody who talks very slowly and you become frustrated, urging them to speed up. Well, if you want to get on to somebody's frequency fast, you can do so immediately by talking at the same speed as them.

Similarly, people talk at different volumes. We can even make sweeping generalisations by nationality. How would you compare the volume of normal speech of a German and a Frenchman? The same rules apply. We all believe that the 'normal' volume for speech is the one that we happen to be talking at. Therefore, if you wish to get on to your future client's frequency, try speaking at the volume he does.

Incidentally, when you are on someone's frequency, in rapport, they are unlikely to notice you pacing them. To them you are talking normally. When I am leading seminars, I always change my tone of voice to match that of a person asking a question. Sometimes other delegates notice the change but the person who asked the question never has, even when discussing tone. Try it yourself to see (and hear) what you find.

Always remember that non-verbal pacing has more influence than tone and language combined. If the prospect talks about his hobby of train-spotting, which you find thoroughly boring, that's great. Non-verbally pace and concentrate on listening to every word and calculate how it can be utilised. You will be developing a deep rapport without saying a word, gaining valuable information on the client's needs, style and interests, which may be used later in achieving the required result.

Now we have another medium that for many is the main communication medium – email. With email, we have taken out the body language and the tonality. The advantage with email is that we have a written record of the language patterns of everyone we communicate with. We can thus analyse them at our leisure unlike telephone or face to face meetings.

Progress now:

How can you develop rapport using the telephone?

How can you develop rapport using e-mail?

C – High-level pacing

At the highest level of our minds are our beliefs, values and identity. Pacing at this level can be very profound indeed as these areas are by definition the most important part of us, determining our behaviour in any situation. As they are so important, pacing someone else in these areas might cause internal conflict with your own beliefs, value and identity. Let us have a brief look at each in turn.

Identity:
- I am ...
- I am a Christian, British, a creative entrepreneur, a father, an author, a results-focused coach ...

What identity or identities are important for you?

Values and Customs
For men, wearing a suit, collar and tie, and short hair is the only acceptable form of dress, is an example of a value in the corporate world. Dress code can vary between sector and company. Wearing smart casual to a sales visit won't work here!

Beliefs
'You get what you pay for,' or, *'Watch the pennies and the pounds will look after themselves'*.

These types of beliefs tend to be deep and thus are difficult to change. I therefore suggest matching them; show how your proposal conforms to the belief and is in accordance with it.

Corporate culture, a mixture of all the above, is usually a high level of rapport where one can identify with the group. Those of you who have teenage children will know just how powerful group psychology can be. Or is it just coincidence that they happen to like the same clothes, foods, pop stars and places all at the same time! Behavioural studies have long shown us how powerful peer pressure to conform in a group can be. When the informal rules for conformity are established, anyone not abiding with them will simply not fit in. Corporate culture manifests itself in terms of dress, style of suit, tie and so on, attitudes, how superiors are addressed (Sir, Mr McMillan or Alex). In the army, calling your immediate superior by his first name won't go down well; in an advertising agency it would. One might expect more formality in a firm of accountants in the City than in the same firm's office in the provinces. The point is that, more important than dressing as smartly as you can (and sometimes contrary to it), you should match your style of dress to that of the organisation you are visiting.

In China and Japan, it is customary for all staff to start the day by singing the company song. What a way to get the team in total rapport – identity, values, beliefs, physiology, tone and language all at the same time!

The business lunch is a good opportunity to gain some very easy rapport-enhancing points. Have you ever gone to lunch with someone and had a pint of lager while they drank Perrier water? You are out of frequency with that person. You then order steak pie, chips and beans and they have a cheese sandwich. The disrapport that something like this creates is quite strong. People have a natural tendency to feel happy when they are like you. Have you heard the conversations of people in the bar discussing food or wine? Notice the amount of times you hear 'I will if you will'. This could mean taking wine or not with the meal. Now, armed with this knowledge, ask your future client what they would like to drink first and match it. Find out what they are eating first and order something similar. This will get you far closer to getting their business than, for example, trying to impress them by insisting that you pay.

In a previous partnership, we had offices in the City and in Sussex. A client lunch in the City was typically a bottle of quality wine in a classy restaurant. A client lunch in Sussex was typically a beer and a pie in a pub. In the City, clients want to get straight down to business. In Sussex, clients want to get to know you better and do not wish to be hurried. If there is so much difference in behaviour within 30 miles, imagine the variety of someone who transacts business internationally! Find out what they would prefer (all you need do is ask) and be flexible in your style to match theirs. (For a much deeper and creative approach to dealing with business people abroad, see *The Business Chameleon*, by Ron Roet and Diana Beaver, Management Books 2000 Ltd, 2003)

Consider that your future clients must communicate with you in some way. Therefore, there is always enough communication to develop rapport and the only situation where you cannot develop rapport is when one of you turns your back and exits.

Additionally, consider that the rapport techniques in this and the previous chapters have been developed from NLP practitioners, a large range of communicators enjoying formidable results. When practised and developed to a high degree, these advanced, yet simple rapport skills produce incredible results in seconds.

Progress now:

Think of your three top clients. How would you define their corporate culture?

D – The hierarchy of rapport

Below is a summary of what you can mirror to establish rapport.

Personality
Identity
Values
Beliefs

Physiological
Posture
Breathing
Blinking
Nodding
Movements

Tonality
Volume
Pitch
Rhythm
Speed
Accent

Language
Buzzwords
Predicates
Jargon
Slang
Expressions
Phrases
Metaphors
Sensory Language System

E – Moving on once rapport is established

Once you have rapport, and that need only take up to a minute, you are in a position to lead to wherever you want to go. You are 'hooking them' on to you with your pacing. You are respecting their present world by talking to them in it. Following your lead, they will increasingly adapt your tone of voice after you speak. If this does not happen, you have not established a strong enough state of rapport. No problem, just go back to stage one. When you have a high level of rapport, the client (for he will no longer be a prospect) is likely to say something along the lines of, 'You know, you and I are very alike,' or 'we are kindred spirits'.

If rapport is about getting on the same frequency as your future client, the next stage is to listen, gathering information, then lead the conversation into matching client needs to offering and finally of course, to closing the deal. You lead the conversation by well-directed questions. Then ask for the business.

10

How to Listen and Profit from What You Hear

'People want economy and they will pay any price to get it.'
Lee Iacocca

'Well I told you once and I told you twice, but you never listen to my advice. You don't try very hard to please me, with what you know, it should be easy.'　Mick Jagger

'Look, if you had one shot, one opportunity, to seize everything you ever wanted – in one moment, would you capture it or just let it slip.'　Eminem

This chapter ...

A　What influences you?
B　Are we talking the same language?
C　A closer look at 'native' language
D　'Pictures' language customers
E　'Feelings' language customers
F　'Logic' language customers
G　'Sounds' language customers
H　'Smells and tastes' language customers
I　It's all in the eyes!
J　Where do the eyes go?
K　Typical characteristics of 'native' language speakers
L　Examples of multi-lingual sales lines
M　A second look at what influences you

A – What influences you?

Imagine being in a room with someone, and £20 notes flutter down from the ceiling continuously. That is how I see a client visit, but you need to be willing to listen carefully for it to happen.

Have you ever listened to a personal development audio recording? Have you observed that if you repeat the experience, you notice things that you did not the first time around, and notice new things each time you play it. Play a CD to someone and, after five minutes, ask them to report on exactly what they heard. You might be surprised how little that is. In selling, when you talk to someone, somewhere in what they are saying is the doorway to making them a customer. You just have to find it and walk through. The key to that door is your listening skills. It is as though they have a silver platter stacked high with wads of £20 notes, saying 'please help yourself to as many of these as you want'. As I prove in one of my seminars, if anyone talks for three minutes on any subject at all, the information is there on how to get them to bring out the silver platter!

To listen, all you have to do is shut up internally and externally. The second part means that you have to focus on them and not have any thoughts or internal dialogue in any other direction. This is just a matter of forming a new habit. With a recruitment business I was running, I once helped my team to develop this habit. I recorded their phone calls and paid them a sales performance bonus on the following basis: For every sentence they spoke, I deducted £1 and for every sentence the other person spoke, I gave them 25 pence. Sales went up! Not only that, but my sales staff reported that selling was a lot easier than they thought.

For example, people will mark out what is important to them by changing their voice tone in some way. Even if you start the meeting asking about the holiday they have just returned from, much is to be gained. Firstly their values will become apparent, their attitude to price relative to quality and value for money, how they come to decisions, their personality, who and what is important in their lives. When you get down to business, you will start with all this information and, with a well directed conversation, have them in a good mood already. All done on safe ground.

When you have got in the habit of listening, you then have to analyse what you hear relative to your objectives. Language is in fact a complex digital software code. Like any piece of software, it is full of patterns. In our spoken or written word, there are many patterns. Many of these patterns are not hard to find if you know how to look for them. When you know somebody's key communication patterns, selling to them becomes very easy. When somebody talks they will be sending out clear 'buying signals' that will tell you exactly what you have to do to sell to them. For this chapter, I have covered a major common pattern in detail for you to learn and practice with. There are many others. Let us start with a self-analysis before we use our new skills on others.

Progress now:

Complete the following questionnaire, coding as follows.
>   4 = Closest to describing you
>   3 = Next best
>   2 = Not particularly you
>   1 = Least like you

1. I make important decisions based on:

- ◆ gut level feelings   a☐
- ◆ which way sounds best   b☐
- ◆ what looks best to me   c☐
- ◆ precise review and study of the issues   d☐

2. Whilst listening to a presentation, I am most likely to be influenced by:

- ◆ the other person's tone of voice   a☐
- ◆ whether or not I can see the other person's argument   b☐
- ◆ the logic of the other person's points   c☐
- ◆ being in touch with the issues   d☐

3. I am happiest when:

- ◆ I am listening to music   a☐
- ◆ I have balanced my personal budget   b☐
- ◆ going for a walk on a sunny day   c☐
- ◆ watching a good movie   d☐

(continued)

4. *My main motivation to exercise and keep fit is:*

- it would make me feel better   a ☐
- it would make me look better   b ☐
- a class with music to supply rhythm   c ☐
- improved performance in my business   d ☐

5. *If I bought a pet it would be because:*

- they are warm and cuddly   a ☐
- their sound is very welcoming   b ☐
- they look just lovely   c ☐
- I can make money from breeding them   d ☐

6. *Are you more receptive to people who:*

- are very precise in their communication   a ☐
- have a pleasant friendly voice   b ☐
- dress well and look smart   c ☐
- give you a firm handshake   d ☐

7. *I communicate how I am at any time by:*

- the way I dress and look   a ☐
- the feelings I share with friends   b ☐
- the words I choose   c ☐
- the tone of my voice   d ☐

8. *It is easiest for me to:*

- find the ideal volume and tuning on a stereo system   a ☐
- select the most intellectually relevant point   b ☐
- select the most comfortable furniture   c ☐
- select rich, attractive, colour combinations   d ☐

9. *I am very:*

- responsive to the decorations in a room   a ☐
- tuned to the sounds of my surroundings   b ☐
- adept at making sense of new facts and data   c ☐
- sensitive to clothes on my body   d ☐

(continued)

10. When I buy my dream car I will be most influenced by:

• how it looks, colour, design etc   a☐
• the sensation of speed from behind the wheel   b☐
• the quality of the stereo and quietness of engine   c☐
• the best deal I can get   d☐

Now transfer your scores to the following matrix:

	Pictures (P)	Feelings (F)	Logic (L)	Sounds (S)
1	c	a	d	b
2	b	d	c	a
3	d	c	b	a
4	b	a	d	c
5	c	a	d	b
6	c	d	a	b
7	a	b	c	d
8	d	c	b	a
9	a	d	c	b
10	a	b	d	c
Total				

(Note that the smell and taste sensory languages are not separately included in this test as they are considered less significant, and are often included in 'Feelings' for these purposes)

My language preference order is:

First =   Second =

Third =   Fourth =

B – Are we talking the same language?

Four entrepreneurs met on a business start-up course and, after talking, realised that they had each just come back from holiday. They related their holidays to each other, as represented below. Which one appeals to you the most?

The first person, Tracy, said that her resort was beautiful. There were panoramic views of an attractive coastline and it was sunny every day. The sea was a deep shade of green, contrasting with a picturesque sky of light blue. The town itself was attractive with lots to see of interest. Tracy took her boyfriend and said that when they returned they both looked very good with attractive tans. She imagined that they would be going back there next year.

Sharon spent all of her holiday enjoying various sports, particularly water sports, which she described as giving you a tremendous feeling with the sun on your face, the wind in your hair and an exhilaration from speed felt all over the body. She went dancing most evenings and ate, drank and partied non-stop.

George had chosen his resort after careful analysis of the alternatives to ensure best value for money. He reckoned that his chosen resort offered the best all-round package and he was not disappointed. He made a clear plan of what he wanted to do, which involved a great deal of diverse activities. He studied all the tours available to avoid repetition and scheduled them in with periods of complete rest and relaxation.

Peter said that his resort was lively and they spent most evenings listening to local musicians with the background sound of the surf breaking. The traffic was a bit noisy but the hotel was situated in a quiet part of the town. He chose this holiday because of a friend's recommendation, which was supported by what he was told by the travel agent.

The above holidays could all be the same resort. Tracy clearly prefers pictures, Sharon feelings, George logic and Peter sounds. The one that appealed to you the most gives a good orientation as to your mix of preferences.

Sometimes we do not seem to be speaking the same language. From a sensory point of view, this could be literally correct. Good communication skills bridge these differences and provide flexibility, which is the mother of influence.

C – A closer look at 'native' language

Our experiences are structured in terms of our senses. When we think or process information internally, we either use one of the sensory languages or the one non-sensory language, which we call the logic mode. These five different languages can be directly compared to spoken languages, such as Spanish, Greek or Japanese. If you were selling to a Japanese, you would probably do better by speaking Japanese and even better using the style, customs and manner of a Japanese. This way you will literally be speaking his language and therefore develop rapport and communicate far more easily with him.

The same principle applies to the 'languages of the mind' and you are already conversant in all of them as we all speak all of these languages some of the time. However, for most people, one language is predominant, and doing nothing more than talking to someone in their preferred language will virtually guarantee your getting your message through. The languages are:

- Pictures
- Feelings
- Logic
- Sounds
- Smell/taste

There are now two simple things to do

1. Establish which language somebody is predominantly using. This can be done by any one of the following methods, using the others for confirmation:
   (a) Listen to the words and phrases repeatedly used.
   (b) Notice their body shape, which can be a key indicator.
   (c) Observe certain involuntary eye movements.
   (d) Observe breathing patterns.

2. Talk to them in their language:
   (a) Use the words and phrases of their language, particularly the same ones.
   (b) Mirror their physiology, which will be strongly influenced by their 'native' language.
   (c) Show 'pictures people' things, (brochures, charts, references, reports, pictures etc); talk to 'sounds people' about what other customers

have said. Let 'feelings people' touch your product and try it out; explain to 'logic people' the arguments in favour of your products.

As an interesting exercise to illustrate the need to be completely flexible, imagine that you are a car salesman and consider how you may differently approach each type of customer.

D – 'Pictures' language customers

Vocabulary

Black/white	Bright	Blank	Clear	Colour	
Dim	Dark	Dream	Eye	Focus	Gleam
Glowing	Golden	Hazy	Hindsight	Horizon	Image
Imagine	Insight	Illusion	Look	Luminous	Opaque
Outlook	Perspective	Picture	Reflect	Scene	Shady
Shine	Translucent	Transparent	View	Vision	Visualise
Vivid					

Phrases/Metaphors:

I cannot face it
Looking at the big picture
It's not exactly black and white to me
I need to distance myself from the problem
He's had a colourful past
She has a sunny disposition
Looks alright to me
I cannot seem to focus on what you are saying
That puts a bit more light on it
That's brightened up my day
It all seems very hazy
I see what you mean
I want a different perspective
Let us look at this closely
I can picture what you are saying
I can see right through your argument
Show me what you mean
Things are looking up

It appears that you are right

Seeing eye to eye

Turn a blind eye

Progress now:

Construct five questions to ask 'pictures' people.

1.

2.

3.

4.

5.

E – 'Feelings' language customers

Vocabulary

Cold	Contact	Firm	Flow	Grasp	Handle
Hassle	Hold	Itching	Lift	Loose	Move
Pressure	Pushy	Rub	Sensitive	Sharp	Shrug
Smooth	Soft	Solid	Sticky	Support	Tackle
Tepid	Texture	Thrust	Tickle	Tight	Tired
Touch	Turn	Uptight	Warm	Weight	

Phrases/Metaphors:

I am ready to tackle this head on

I've got a good feeling about this

He needs to get a grip on his results

He is as solid as a rock

It is a rather sticky situation

I need a concrete proposal

You hurt his feelings

A cool customer

Can you give me a hand

Things just seemed to flow smoothly

He rubs me up the wrong way

That company needs to pull itself together

I can grasp what you are saying

Can you hold on a minute?

I feel it in my bones

One step at a time

Hot-headed

A pat on the back

Boils down to

Tied up

Progress now:

Construct five questions to ask 'feelings' people.

1.

2.

3.

4.

5.

F – 'Logic' language customers

Vocabulary

Analyse	Arrange	Assess	Balancing	Basis	Believe
Breakdown	Calculate	Cogitate	Compute	Conceive	Conclude
Conjecture	Consider	Criticise	Critique	Decide	Deliberate
Dissect	Estimate	Enquire	Evaluate	Examine	Explain
Figure	Gauge	Guess	Investigate	Judgement	Know
Logic	Measure	Mentality	Muse	Notice	Number
Perceive	Ponder	Rank	Rational	Reason	Reckon
Remember	Review	Scrutinise	Sense	Sift	Study
Suppose	Surmise	Survey	Systematic	Testing	Think
Understand	Validate	Work Out			

Phrases/Metaphors:

I would like to think about it

Consider it done

Common sense

Let me think about it

Seems logical to me

I reckon your right

I understand what you mean

I guess it adds up to a good deal

Progress now:

Construct five questions to ask 'logic' people.

1.

2.

3.

4.

5.

G – 'Sounds' language customers

Vocabulary

Call	Chatter	Chirpy	Clash	Click
Deaf	Dissonant	Drum	Dumb	Harmony
Hear	Hearsay	Language	Loud	Melody
Monotonous	Patter	Question	Rhythm	Ring
Say	Sing	Speech	Talk	Tell
Tinkle	Tone	Tune	Unheard of	Wavelength

Phrases/Metaphors:

We are on the same wavelength

Speaking the same language

Tune in to this

I hear what you are saying
Music to my ears
I like what you are saying
Lost for words
Living in harmony
Talking gobbledygook
Noise in the system
Quiet as a mouse
Sounds good to me
Turn a deaf ear
Tone it down
Rings a bell
Strikes a chord
Struck dumb
Calling the tune
Loud and clear
I have heard a whisper
I keep telling him
It's come to a screeching halt
Rumour has it

Progress now:

Construct five questions to ask 'sounds' people.

1.

2.

3.

4.

5.

H – 'Smells/tastes' language customers

Vocabulary

Acrid	Appetite	Aroma	Bite	Bitter	Bland
Bouquet	Chew	Crisp	Fishy	Flavour	Fragrant
Fresh	Gorge	Juicy	Luscious	Nibble	Nosey
Reek	Savour	Scent	Smell	Sniff	Spicy
Stinks	Swallow	Sweet	Tasty	Whiff	

Phrases/Metaphors:

Seems a bit fishy to me

The sweet taste/smell of success

He is stinking rich

Taking a sugar-coated pill

He has a good nose for business

He's all sour grapes

It makes the spice of life

He has bitten off more than he can chew

I'd like to get a bite of that apple

He came out of that deal smelling of roses

Our northern branch is a smooth running operation

I need to get to the meat of the proposal

I'd like a better price for starters

Too many cooks spoil the broth

If you do not like the heat get out of the kitchen

Progress now:

Construct five questions to ask 'smells/tastes' people.

1.

2.

3.

4.

5.

I – It's all in the eyes!

When we are not consciously looking at something we move our eyes according to what language we are operating internally. There are exceptions to this rule but they are rare (The main exceptions are left-handed people. In their case the opposite direction is usually found).

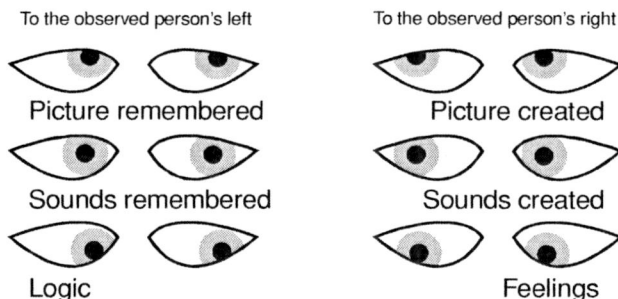

To the observed person's left   To the observed person's right

Picture remembered   Picture created

Sounds remembered   Sounds created

Logic   Feelings

Looking At Someone

The central position usually means that the person is accessing different 'languages' at the same time. Remember that this is a generalisation and it is always best to calibrate for the individual. These movements are unconscious and indicate where the 'unconscious' mind is, the conscious mind could be elsewhere.

J – Where do the eyes go?

When people access a different sensory part of the brain, unconsciously they tend to make an eye direction movement reflecting where they are focused. Thus by observing their eyes you can tell what sensory mode they are in. For example, if they are visualising, then talking in that mode will be more appropriate. You will be surprised at just how clear these movements are and why you never noticed it before.

	To your left (their right)	To your right (their left)
Up	Pictures created (PC)	Pictures remembered (PR)
Central	Sounds created (HC)	Sounds remembered (HR)
Down	Feelings (F)	Logic (C)

(Note that these observations are as you see them – the movements you see as towards the left are actually to the other person's right.)

Progress now:

Put the following questions to at least three people and without telling them what you are doing, record where their eyes go.

● What does your house look like?

Eyes: Up / Central / Down / Left / Right

● What does your favourite Disney character look like?

Eyes: Up / Central / Down / Left / Right

● What would your dream car look like?

Eyes: Up / Central / Down / Left / Right

● Picture yourself driving a red Ferrari?

Eyes: Up / Central / Down Left / Right

● What was the last sentence you spoke?

Eyes: Up / Central / Down / Left / Right

● What does Donald Duck sound like?

Eyes: Up / Central / Down / Left / Right

● Imagine the voice of your last prospect?

Eyes: Up / Central / Down / Left / Right

● What would your best friend sound like talking Japanese?

Eyes: Up / Central / Down / Left / Right

● What does 3 + 12 - 7 + 5 make?

Eyes: Up / Central / Down / Left / Right

● What does £1100 + VAT total?

Eyes: Up / Central / Down / Left / Right
(continued)

160

- What really relaxes you?

  Eyes: Up / Central / Down / Left / Right

- What part of you gets hottest quickest in a sauna?

  Eyes: Up / Central / Down / Left / Right

K – Typical characteristics of 'native' language speakers

To help you in reading people there are other giveaway signs.

Preference – Pictures

These speakers' voices are often high-pitched and slightly breathless. They tend to breathe high in the chest. They often have tension in the neck and shoulders. Voice tempo is often quite quick. 'Pictures' people seldom get lost, if they are in a place once, they will remember the area and find their way back. They typically have photographic memories and can vividly retrieve past scenes with ease. Physical characteristics may be summarised as follows: eyes up, head up, frequent blinking, even closing of eyes. They tend to be thinner and dress well.

Preference – Feelings

'Feelings' people breathe low down in the belly, and accordingly their voices tend to be deeper than the other categories. They tend to speak slowly often with spaces or gaps. Their eyes tend down to the right. They often love sports, use gestures a lot and really enjoy their food.

Preference – Logic

'Logic' people do not trust their basic experiences. They trust the words that describe the experiences instead. This gives them a cautious outlook, as they search for the perfect description.

Preference – Sounds

They often speak well and rhythmically. They are constantly talking to themselves in internal dialogue. In fact they are often hard to close on as they won't turn off the internal dialogue. They tend to breathe in the middle of the chest. This gives them a rhythmic tempo. As you can imagine they like listening to music or attending concerts. Their eyes tend to be level left and right. They will often hum or whistle.

Progress now:

Think of people that you deal with a lot. Which categories do they fit into?

L – Examples of multi-lingual sales lines

Pictures:

If I could show you an attractive benefit, you would want at least to look at it, wouldn't you?

Imagine in your mind's eye owning this product.

Can you see what I am getting at?

Can you visualise the benefits of this product?

Can I focus you on these particular features?

You should see this as a golden opportunity.

Does this reflect your requirements?

Feelings:

If this feels good to you, I can pull some strings for delivery Monday.

Can you get a feel for what I am saying?

Can I touch base with you next week?

We have to stick to the full price on this one.

It takes all the hassle out of buying.

Logic:

Considering the arguments, what do you think?

Do you want me to investigate further?

What do you reckon?

It is the only logical choice.

The figures add up, don't they?

Sounds:

If I could tell you a way in which you could benefit, you would at least want to hear about it, wouldn't you?

How does that sound?

Listen to this quote from John Smith of ABC Systems.

Are we on the same wavelength?

Tell me what you think?

Have you changed your tune?

Smells/Tastes:

Sniffing out opportunities.

Taste of his own medicine.

The deal on the new lease stinks.

Losing that contract was rotten luck.

That way of doing business I find distasteful.

M – A second look at what influences you

Write down five sentences of things that you like or dislike strongly. Be sure to describe exactly what it is that you like or dislike.

1.

2.

3.

4.

5.

Now go through the above underlining the Pictures, Feelings, Logic and Sounds words and add them up. Check the results with the test at the beginning of this chapter to confirm your personal profile.

	Pictures	Feelings	Logic	Sounds
Totals	_____	_____	_____	_____

I never go into a sales presentation with a pre-planned structure. My mind is completely at a blank when I go in. My antennae are fully out to listen and observe, to gain information to make a decision as to how to go forward. Listening actually is harder work than talking, although to a casual observer you don't seem to be doing much at all!

11

Turning Objections Into Benefits Through Verbal Aikido

'You cannot have a negative and a positive thought at the same time so you may as well have a positive one.'
Robert Stevanowski, Co-Founder of A.C.N.

'Don't find a fault; find a remedy.'   Henry Ford

'Well I stand up next to a mountain, and I chop it down with the edge of my hand.'   Jimi Hendrix

This chapter ...

A   Let us look at objections in your business
B   What is verbal Aikido, why is it different?
C   The objection to benefit matrix
D   Benefits/dangers of negatives
E   The power of parallel story telling
F   The power of visualising what you want to say
G   Word play
H   Presuppositions
I   The agreement frame
J   Getting through secretaries and other gatekeepers
K   Magic selling words

A – Let us look at objections in your business

Think of three objections that you regularly come up against when selling your services, write these in section A. In section B enter how you currently deal with the objection. Leave section C blank for the moment (we will be coming back to this at the end of the chapter).

1. A.

   B.

   C.

2. A.

   B.

   C.

3. A.

   B.

   C.

B – What is verbal Aikido, why is it different?

Verbal Aikido is a method of objection management that avoids head-on clashes and utilises the power of the objection in our response. This is done by gaining access to something that already exists. It gets future clients to look at something differently – not differently *our* way, but differently *their* way. That is why it is so powerful a technique. The most important thing to remember is that everything is relative – an event only has meaning to an individual in the context of his or her own experiences and assumptions. Change the context or the assumptions and you change the meaning.

For Example:
What does heavy rain signify?
> Bad news if you have the washing out.

Good news if you are a farmer suffering drought.
> Bad news if you are having a garden party.

Good news if you are at sea, without water.
> Bad news if you have just polished the car.

Good news if your house is on fire.
> Bad news if you slip over.

Good news if you sell umbrellas.
> ... and so on

The meaning of any event depends on how you look at it. When you change how you look at it, the meaning can also change. When meaning changes, so can responses and behaviour. Therefore, developing the skill of applying Verbal Aikido to events or situations in the prospect's mind (that is, changing the way the prospect looks at the events or situations) will give you greater freedom and choices within the prospect's model of the world. This is because the 'event' or 'concern' itself has been totally respected, therefore so will the new way of looking at their objection. Or to put it more simply, every cloud has a silver lining – if you look for it you will find it.

Imagine that a future client says to you, *'Your price is too high.'* Ever had that experience? We tend to add our meaning to that statement, which is often quite different from the meaning intended. It could mean any of the following, for example:

He believes he is not getting value for money.
He wants something for nothing.
He does not know what prices involve or include.
He thinks that he cannot afford it.
He can get the same service more cheaply.
He hasn't made comparisons.

He is out for a discount.
Benefits plus Service equals Price does not add up.
It is his job to say that.
He wants to know more.
He is testing you to see how you react.
It is the first thing that came into his head.
He may have a fixed budget in mind.
His previous purchase was cheaper.
He has had a recent bad service experience.
He wants to hear why he should pay this price.
It is a total red herring.

It could mean any of the above and a whole lot more. So, before we deal with an objection, we must ascertain what exactly he means. Depending on what he means will determine the best response.

Verbal Aikido responses are therefore found by asking these questions:

- 'How can this objection/limitation/problem be turned to advantage?'
- 'What is the useful value of this statement/opinion/comment/behaviour/fact?'

It is not enough to satisfy the prospect on an objection. Our objective is to actually turn it into an advantage. Therefore, objections should be received with relish as they will offer a short cut to a deal. Your future client will be given more ways to look at problems, and the more ways you look at problems the more solutions there will be. The really adept sales people lead the future client to these solutions rather than providing them. This way he answers his own objections in the way that is most meaningful and acceptable for him.

To save time, I have classified thirteen techniques of Verbal Aikido. In different circumstances for different future clients, some will lead to a better outcome than others. It depends on the specific circumstances but they generally fall broadly into two categories. The first is where the context is changed and the second is where the interpretation of the meaning is changed.

Remember that the effect of the above will be stronger if you have developed a deep rapport. The responses can begin with the following to maintain rapport:

'I appreciate that, and ...'

'I agree, and...'
'I respect that, and...'
'That's right, and...'

(Remember that disagreeing with matching body language will give stronger rapport than agreeing with mismatching body language.)

C – The objection to benefit matrix

On the next two pages are worked examples of the thirteen approaches to Verbal Aikido. The examples lists thirteen different responses to turn first a 'pricing' objection and then a 'no-change objection' into a benefit. The actual choice of response will vary according to the context and the particular future client. Work through the examples for each heading, appreciating what is likely to happen in the future client's mind with each response. Consider where the conversation and his thoughts are being led. Then when you feel comfortable with the worked examples, go to the next page and put in the first objection you listed in section A at the beginning of this chapter. Complete the list of alternative responses. When you have finished this, do the same on the following pages for the other two objections you listed. You will soon find that you begin to appreciate exactly why this approach is so powerful.

I have classified thirteen approaches for every objection you are likely to have to deal with. Below I give a worked example of each approach for the common objection, 'Your prices are too high'. Remember, if somebody says this, it does suggest that they are interested.

Redefine their statement:
'Expense is relative, it all depends on where you are coming from.'

Assume a positive intention:
'You are looking then for best value for money.'

Look for a counter example:
'Have you bought something expensive before and been satisfied.'

Tell a parallel story that brings them to a different conclusion:
'I bought a cheap car once, it broke down! I'll never do that again.'

That is only one view of the world, there are others:
'In comparison to what?'

Change the time frame:
'Time will show the full story.'

Point out other evidence and opinions:
'With respect that is your belief.'

Move the conversation to a higher level where you can get agreement:
Aren't most things expensive these days?

Move the conversation to a lower level to clarify and confirm the details:
'What aspect of our service specifically do you think is too highly priced?'

Elicit their values and decision criterion:
'What exactly are you looking for?'

Look for their objective and needs:
'What are your objectives exactly?'

Point out the positive consequences of buying:
'The quality of your products will improve.'

Point out the negative consequences of not buying:
'So you might miss an opportunity worth having.'

Here is another worked example for you to consider, responding to the objection: 'It is difficult to change suppliers'.

Redefine their statement:
'It's not really difficult, it just requires thinking through.'

Assume a positive intention:
'You will presumably consider all the options carefully then.'

Look for a counter example:
'Has any successful decision you have made not been difficult in some way?'

Tell a parallel story that brings them to a different conclusion:
'I have been finding it difficult to change my diet and lose weight. Yet I know it is a change for the better and must not let old habits restrict my future.'

That is only one view of the world, there are others:
'That's just your perception. In reality you may not find it as difficult as you think.'

Change the time frame:
'With hindsight haven't many previous changes turned out easier than you thought?'

Point out other evidence and opinions:
'Believing that makes it seem difficult.'

Move the conversation to a higher level where you can get agreement:
'Most worthwhile changes are difficult.'

Move the conversation to a lower level to clarify and confirm the details:
'Only the first step is difficult.'

Elicit their values and decision criterion:
'How have you got over this previously?'

Look for their objective and needs:
'It's difficult to get the best prices and service.'

Point out the positive consequences of buying:
'That ensures we will respect winning your business.'

Point out the negative consequences of not buying:
'Present suppliers can take your custom for granted.'

Progress now:

Now take your first objection from Section A, and write it here

•

Redefine their statement:
Response:

Assume a positive intention:
Response:

Look for a counter example:
Response:

Tell a parallel story that brings them to a different conclusion:
Response:

That is only one view of the world, there are others:
Response:

Change the time frame:
Response:

Point out other evidence and opinions:
Response:

Move the conversation to a higher level where you can get agreement:
Response:

Move the conversation to a lower level to clarify and confirm the details:
Response:

Elicit their values and decision criterion:
Response:

Look for their objective and needs:
Response:

Point out the positive consequences of buying:
Response:

Point out the negative consequences of not buying:
Response:

Progress now:

Now take your second objection from Section A, and write it here

•

Redefine their statement:
Response:

Assume a positive intention:
Response:

Look for a counter example:
Response:

Tell a parallel story that brings them to a different conclusion:
Response:

That is only one view of the world, there are others:
Response:

Change the time frame:
Response:

Point out other evidence and opinions:
Response:

Move the conversation to a higher level where you can get agreement:
Response:

Move the conversation to a lower level to clarify and confirm the details:
Response:

Elicit their values and decision criterion:
Response:

Look for their objective and needs:
Response:

Point out the positive consequences of buying:
Response:

Point out the negative consequences of not buying:
Response:

Progress now:

Now take your third objection from Section A, and write it here

•

Redefine their statement:
Response:

Assume a positive intention:
Response:

Look for a counter example:
Response:

Tell a parallel story that brings them to a different conclusion:
Response:

That is only one view of the world, there are others:
Response:

Change the time frame:
Response:

Point out other evidence and opinions:
Response:

Move the conversation to a higher level where you can get agreement:
Response:

Move the conversation to a lower level to clarify and confirm the details:
Response:

Elicit their values and decision criterion:
Response:

Look for their objective and needs:
Response:

Point out the positive consequences of buying:
Response:

Point out the negative consequences of not buying:
Response:

D – Benefits/dangers of negatives

In your conversation, take care when using negative words. There are two dangers. The first is that negative words suggest mental pictures and sounds and thus feelings. Secondly negatives such as, 'please do not hesitate to call' exist in language, but not in experience. For example, without adding further content, what comes into your mind when you consider 'The customer is not on the phone'. It is difficult to think of something not happening. We usually have to think of it first in the positive in order to consider it. To illustrate this, consider what comes into your mind after reading the following.

Do not think of a cheque in your name for £10,000.

Now, keep not thinking of that cheque.

Chances are you found it hard not to think of it, and quite a nice thought too. The effect is even stronger if heard and not read.

Now consider these – which ones do you think you should use and which ones should you be careful to avoid.

'Do not think that you have to decide today.'
'Do not worry about the price for the moment.'
'It is not expensive.'
'I think you will agree it is not bad.'
'I don't want you to worry about delivery.'
'Do not drink and drive'.
 'Do not walk on the grass.'
'Do not smoke.'
'No entry.'

E – The power of parallel story telling

An analogy (or a metaphor) is a story implying a comparison. Communication through analogy can be a very elegant way of bypassing the conscious processes and influencing the unconscious mind directly. Metaphors are a powerful way of influencing. They can gain, by putting realism through colour, sound and movement into your description. They can add to appeal and effect by introducing emotive imagery or description. Stories are better recalled than bare facts, and at a deeper level.

The 'Third-party quote technique' is an example. *'My previous call was to John Wheeler, the Purchasing Director of Bloggs and Co. He said, "I have tried out your products and despite the fact that they are cheaper than the competition the quality has proved to be better." What do you think of that?'* Somebody else saying it has more influence than your saying, *'I know our prices are cheaper than the competition and that our quality is better.'*

The quotes technique also has the advantage that if it goes wrong in any way, the position is recoverable because the statement is attributed to a third party and not yourself. It is therefore a good way to try out unsure ground to test the response before committing yourself. For example, *'I've just left Peter Higgins of XYZ Ltd, who said to me that the potential of this product is so great you have got to be crazy not to at least try a sample order.'* Less dangerous to try this by using the 'Third-party quote technique', isn't it?

Another method is to make up a longer story introducing analogous characters, places, situations, decisions, etc, to the ones in the current situation; then leading to a solution in the story which the unconscious mind will automatically adapt for the present situation. Hence the term 'parallel story'. This is perhaps more easily explained by example.

Which of the following two narratives makes the point more strongly?

'In life it is best to make a plan and stick to it rigidly. Know clearly where you are going from the outset and do not get diverted on the way. Studies have shown that people who adapt this policy tend to do better in their career than people who do not.'

'A friend of mine went into Victoria Station and approached the ticket booth with a fifty pound note in his hand. He said, 'I would like to go somewhere really nice and attractive. I am not really sure where but I am very determined to arrive.' The ticket clerk looked at my friend and said, 'If you don't know exactly where you want to go how do you expect us to get you there?'

Design parallel stories that are tailored to fit the problem of your clients. Future clients will have unfulfilled desires because of limitations in their model of the world. You can create specific parallel stories that expand the range of the future client's world and guide him to fruitful outcomes.

There are several ways to make a parallel story that helps you win sales.

1. Examine the challenge/objection.
2. Identify all nouns/processes.
3. Select content of story.

4. Create a noun/process in the story for each noun/process in the challenge.
5. Design the story ending for a desired response.

It is not necessary to think on your feet; all you have to do is prepare up to five worked-out and rehearsed stories that will parallel and deal effectively with any objections that you are likely to come across in your sales visits.

You could also design stories that use one of the main 'languages' referred to already in this book using the phrases outlined earlier.

> I have a client, Eurodrive Car Rental Ltd, and like Victor Kiam with his excellent razor, I was so impressed with them I bought shares in the company! On a recent visit I overheard a sales call being made by one of their staff.
>
> '... the Purchasing Manager of a local company, just down the road from you, recently wanted to rent several cars for visiting overseas executives. He eventually chose us at Eurodrive Car Rental Ltd and he told me why. He looked at more than half a dozen leading companies and considered what they had to offer and what he thought of their service. He analysed their prices, guarantees and service differences. The more he probed, the more information there was to compare and the harder a decision became. He asked his MD for his opinion. 'In my experience, I have found that the best strategy in the long run is to choose the company where the staff in your opinion have the maximum integrity, honesty, etc. Then when they make a claim on a benefit you can believe it to be true. You usually get what you pay for and lower prices often mean lower quality somewhere. Therefore go for value for money and not lowest price. Be wary of quotes that have all sorts of hidden extras to be added to them. After-sales service is important and best judged from the quality of the people in the company. The Puchasing Manager later the same day placed his order via the web site at www.eurodrive.com.'

Expressing yourself by putting pictures into the client's mind is a very powerful way of communicating your message. It can also be done in sales letters – as in the following that I use with very successful result:

To: John Smith
The Managing Director
ABC Company

Dear John

You asked specifically about applying coaching to building an entrepreneurial business. Let me start with a short story, that I know you will enjoy and make the point better for you.

I dreamt last night that I was a salesman who went back in time to the Roman Invasion, taking with me a warehouse full of Cruise missiles. I approached local leaders, communicating the benefits and using all types of closes. It sounded too good to be true, which made them sceptical. They had extensive battle experience, believed that they knew everything and that I was trying to dress up old products in new packaging.

I then woke up and thought about the dilemma of the dream. Our coaching promises to *transform*, not just increase, performance. Nobody was going to be convinced of what I could do for them just by being told about it. They had to see the results.

I decided to offer a presentation for management on their premises, called, 'Contingency Coaching – No result, no fee'.

If you have not experienced the acceleration of coaching to building a business, prepare to change your beliefs on what can be achieved, through profitable experience.

Please ring now to arrange a presentation.

Thank you for your attention.

Yours sincerely,

Alex McMillan   www.alexmcmillan.com

F – The power of visualising what you want to say

When we use metaphor or analogy in short phrases, it can be as powerful as a longer prepared story. If the customer's mind is helped to 'picture' what you are saying, the effect will be several times more powerful. Try replacing the first of each pair of responses listed below with the second (i.e. replacing a with b). Reading through you will start to see (literally) why response b is more influential. Learn a few by heart and get into the habit of using them – you will be startled at how persuasive and clear you become to your recipient.

a) I will try hard.

    b) I will give it my best shot.

a) You cannot refuse this offer.

    b) Don't look a gift horse in the mouth.

a) Try it and see.

    b) The proof of the pudding is in the eating.

a) There must be some advantage.

    b) Every cloud has a silver lining.

a) You should prepare for all eventualities.

    b) To have more than one string to one's bow.

a) Working hard.

    b) To be going full swing.

a) It is not difficult.

    b) It's as easy as falling off a log.

a) No real gain.

    b) To rob Peter to pay Paul.

a) Let us both work on it.

    b) Two heads are better than one.

a) I think you are overemphasising the importance.

    b) To make a mountain out of a molehill.

a) I know that it is true.

    b) To stake one's life on it.

a) Uncommitted

    b) To sit on the fence.

a) The same situation.

    b) To be in the same boat.

a) I will listen.

    b) I am all ears.

a) More than one benefit here.

    b) To kill two birds with one stone.

a) To ignore what is going on.

    b) To bury one's head in the sand.

a) Do not take the risk.

    b) A closed mouth catches no flies.

a) Take action at the right time.

    b) Strike whilst the iron is hot.

a) It's better not to procrastinate.

    b) Never put off until tomorrow what you can do today.

a) To waste money.

    b) To throw money down the drain.

a) It might seem better with closer inspection.

    b) To judge a book by its cover.

a) Take a chance and you will probably win.

    b) Fortune favours the brave.

a) Do something about it.

    b) Actions speak louder than words.

a) I agree.

    b) Great minds think alike.

a) It could be the same again.

    b) History repeats itself.

a) Let me be totally honest.

    b) To put ones cards on the table.

a) The wrong way round.

    b) To put the cart before the horse.

a) A certain success should not be put at risk.

    b) A bird in the hand is worth two in the bush.

a) If you want to win you have got to take a risk.

    b) Nothing ventured, nothing gained.

a) Best to be quick.

    b) The early bird catches the worm.

a) Do not be impatient.

    b) Rome was not built in a day.

a) To make contact.

    b) To break the ice.

a) It will increase quickly.

    b) To spread like wildfire.

a) To continue along the same path.

    b) To keep the ball rolling.

a) Be careful.

    b) To see how the land lies.

a) Be careful

    b) All that glisters is not gold.

Think of situations where the following might be used to make your communication more influential:

    To kill the goose that lays the golden eggs.

There are plenty of fish in the sea.
A bird in the hand is worth two in a bush.
To let the cat out of the bag.
To see which way the wind blows.
To stand on one's own two feet.
A lot of water has passed under the bridge.
Look before you leap.
You can't have your cake and eat it.
You are pushing against an open door.

G – Word play

There are many ways in which we are subtly influenced or can influence. If you have something really worthwhile to offer and have a passion for it, then you first need to inform people it is available and match its benefits to their needs. Communication is best kept simple, clear and straightforward. For the written word there are some interesting techniques.

Notice how the underlined parts of the sentences links two separate ideas, which are not necessarily linked.

'I see that you have read the brochure <u>and</u> are ready to decide.'
The conjunction connects the reading of the brochure to the decision process.

'<u>As you read</u> the brochure, <u>you will notice</u> how relevant the product is to your needs.'
Connects reading to the assumption that the product is relevant and that you will figure out yourself in what way. Encourages you to keep looking until you have made the connection.

'<u>While you read</u> the brochure, <u>you will probably find</u> things that are useful.'
Connects in the same way as the above sentence but the word probably makes it a softer connection that would be easier to accept.

'<u>When you try out</u> this new line, <u>you will understand</u> why I thought of you.'
Connects trying out with a benefit to the person and adds a touch of mystery and curiosity as an added incentive.

Progress now:

Think of three sentences that you could add to your advising, letters or e-mail signature applying the above ideas:

1.

2.

3.

Consider how you might react if a sales person said the following to you:

'As you consider the alternative products you should be watchful that your decision to buy is only influenced by real value to you, right now.'

Now consider that the speaker puts a stronger emphasis in some way on the words in italics and underlined.

'As *you* consider the alternative products you *should* be watchful that your decision to *buy* is only influenced by real value to you, *right now*.

Personally I am always wary of listening to advertisements. If you want to lose weight, get out of debt, sell the television! This is unethical selling, creating needs in you for what they have to sell. Ethical selling is satisfying a need that is already there when that need being satisfied improves the real quality of life. Next time you go shopping, notice how many 'tricks' retailers use to get you to buy.

- Fashionable teenage/twenty-something clothing, for example, that is designed to be outdated in three months, long before it wears out.
- Folded garments in a stack so that you struggle to refold them properly and are more likely to buy.
- Fancy up-market bags so everyone on the way home can see you as a quality shopper, whilst giving them a free advert.
- Managing customer flow-throughs with wooden floors for the walkways and carpets only around shelving.
- Most common purchases at the back of the store.
- Window displays focused on 25 metres distances to draw you in.

People naturally put greater emphasis, marking out in some way (louder, softer, slower, faster etc) their most important feelings. As you develop your listening skills, you will become increasingly adept at noticing these patterns.

Such techniques however can be used ethically. For example, if you were giving a motivational speech to your team or at a presentation, something like the following might be useful:

'Hello underline{everyone}, take a seat so that you will underline{feel more comfortable} – we will go through some great ideas in a moment and I know that you are underline{interested} and underline{motivated} to hear them underline{right now}.'

Progress now:

1.Record a speaker on the TV for five minutes. Play the recording back several times and try to notice as many patterns as you can.

2. Design a highly motivational line that you can use on many occasions, that improves the mood of the listener.

H – Presuppositions

The following sentences all contain a presupposition, shown in brackets. Note that the statements are not intended as lies but present a more subtle way of transferring information than stating it directly.

'They always prefer my style of presentation.'
    (There is a 'they'.)

'I like companies that give me the 10% discount.'
    (There *are* companies that give 10% discount.)

'If our major PLC customers didn't get next-day service, they would have gone elsewhere.'
    (He has major PLC customers.)

'If none of your competitors drop their prices, I'll give you the order.'
    (There are competitors in the frame.)

'Several of the companies that have spoken to us left their brochures.'
    (Several companies have spoken to them.)

'It was our new price guarantee policy that has maintained us as market leader.'
    (They are market leader.)

'If you decide to go ahead you can cancel for up to a month.'
> (I don't expect that you want to cancel.)

'What you'd like to order is probably from our new product listing.'
> (You'd like to order something.)

'What your competitor can do to get my account is lower their prices.'
> (Your competitor can get my account.)

'If you tell me your best price, I'll decide now.'
> (There exists a 'best' price.)

'If your price is as low as your competitor, we'll go ahead.'
> (Your competitor has a low price, in his opinion.)

'I respect customers who choose our de luxe services.'
> (There exist such customers and de luxe services.)

'If desperate sellers don't get a deal they will drop their price.'
> (Desperate sellers exist.)

'It was our fast service that persuaded your predecessor to order.'
> (Your predecessor ordered from us, and we have a fast service.)

'I think this product line will continue to do well.'
> (It has done well.)

I – The agreement frame

The 'agreement frame' is the result of extensive studies into top performing communicators. Tests have shown that when someone makes this technique a habit, their results significantly increase. When someone says a sentence and then says 'but' or 'however' the message communicated is that they don't believe in what they just said. In selling, if this is stating the prospect's viewpoint, you are setting yourself up for a difficult position, at worse, argument. When on the other hand you get into the habit of using a conjunction, the conversation will flow far more smoothly and, as you have not challenged his comments or objections, your points will be listened to as they build upon what he said. People who are good at winning arguments might do well as barristers, they do not do well in making sales. The technique is simply that, to exchange 'but' or 'however' with 'and'. Thus:

'Yes, but ...'

    becomes: 'Yes, and ...'

'I see what you are saying, however ...'

    becomes: 'I see what you are saying, and ...'

'I appreciate that, but ...'

    becomes: 'I appreciate that, and ...'

'I agree, but ...'

    becomes: 'I agree, and ...'

'I agree with that, however ...'

    becomes: 'I agree that, and ...'

'That's right, but ...'

    becomes: 'That's right and ...'

Consider the following:

Client:	'Frankly, the service we had from your company last time we did business wasn't all that it could have been.'
Entrepreneur 1:	'I appreciate that, but things have changed now and you need not worry anymore.'
Entrepreneur 2:	'I appreciate that, and I will personally do whatever it takes to ensure that you receive the best possible service.'

J – Getting through secretaries and other gatekeepers

Many entrepreneurs at the early stages have to do a lot of selling because, by definition, they do not have a client list yet. Every company has to get a first customer some time. One of the objections you need to overcome to grow your business is getting through to the right people. The first challenge is to decide which companies and companies/individuals are most worthwhile to get through. This often turns out to be senior managers of companies. So, I am often asked how do I get through secretaries and other gatekeepers – people whose job it is to filter calls.

I am asked this question so often and I answer it with another question. Why get through them? Why not recruit them to your objectives? Why not make them an ally and a friend? Why not get them to give you valuable information on who does what and decides what in the organisation? Why not treat them really nicely, with respect, and develop rapport. When you have done that, ask them for their help and advice. Why not have your brochure passed to her boss with the words, 'I spoke to this company and they are very nice people to deal with.'

People want to get through secretaries because they are not decision makers. Well, possibly, but they are definitely decision influencers. Actually in practice you might be surprised how many decisions are left to them.

As soon as you use a 'sales technique', their unconscious is alerted and responds with a 'defensive technique'. If you don't come over as a salesperson you will not be treated as one. People tend to avoid sales people because their focus is to get you to give them money.

People ask me advice on dealing with difficult people. Stop believing that they are difficult or stop dealing with them. NLP defines that the meaning of your communication is the response you get. Take responsibility:

'What are you doing that is making them difficult?'

'What makes you think they are difficult?'

If they are difficult, then having them as a customer will be harder for someone to take their business away from you. The question focuses on their needs – and what they need to do is focus on the needs of the people they are selling to. Stepping into their shoes will show you the way.

K – Magic selling words

The following fifteen words have been found to be the most frequently used by top performing sales professionals. What do you think might happen if you adopted them?

1.	**Discover**
2.	**Good**
3.	**Money**
4.	**Value**
5.	**Guaranteed**
6.	**Health**
7.	**New**
8.	**Proven**
9.	**Your customer's name** (in the same way they address you)
10.	**Results**

11. Safe
12. Save
13. Own
14. Free
15. Best

All positive words have a magical effect. If you use words that conjure up mental pictures, sounds, memories, then this will lead to the reader feeling good. Getting people to feel good is a good start to selling, (unless you are selling life insurance when you want them to feel fear!).

Progress now:

Now, return to the exercise at the beginning of this chapter and complete section C with how you would now respond to the objections in A. You may be surprised at just how many alternatives you could apply to your business.

12

Getting the Decision

'First make sure you are right, then go ahead.'
Davy Crocket

'Acting on a good idea is better than just having a good idea.'
Robert Half

'My formula for success is rise early, work late, and strike oil.'
Paul Getty

This chapter ...

A   Deal making
B   How do customers analyse information in order to make decisions?
C   The main ways of making decisions
D   Developing your ability to sell to preferred decision styles
E   Closing off

A – Deal making

You have targeted and identified your market, made your approaches and developed rapport. You have then listened for needs and matched them to benefits that you offer. Along the way, you dealt with questions and objections whilst maintaining enthusiasm and energy. All that is left now is to finalise the deal. If you have done your job properly, this should be as simple as asking, 'Shall we go ahead then?' or similar. Your whole contact has been leading to this moment where a prospect turns into a customer.

If anything comes up other than yes, then you have to jump back a stage. There must still be some objections or problems holding things back. Be careful here of red herrings. If people do not have the money for example, they are often reticent to say they cannot afford it.

Your actions in the selling situation (what you say and do) are driven by your attitudes (how you think about your work). For this reason, I dislike the term 'sales presentation.' A presentation is a one-way process, a monologue during which you 'present' your products and services to the customer. If you consider your primary task to be that of making presentations, you become predisposed to monopolising the situation by doing more telling than selling. Make it interactive.

Customers rarely discuss their problems, needs and concerns without some urging on your part, and they certainly won't buy unless they believe the benefits you offer will satisfy their needs. To help customers achieve this understanding, you must involve them in the selling process and engage them in productive dialogue. Simply talking to your customers does nothing but keep the focus on you, effectively removing them from the selling equation. *Any sales approach that ignores the customer is doomed to failure from the start.*

B – How do customers analyse information in order to make decisions?

You need to size up future clients and tailor your presentations to their individual buying strategy. You should have been looking to give away clues to how they come to decisions from the first time they spoke to you.

Traditionally, people promoting their business create empathy with prospective customers by finding out what their future customer is interested in and then talking about that. Let us say their interest is baseball.

Fortunately, I was taken to a baseball match by a Texan friend of mine, Mike Spiller, to see the Astros play in Houston and had it all explained to me. So I would now be comfortable to talk on this subject. If on the other hand you have never been to a baseball game in your life, the conversation would be one-sided at best.

Establishing decision-making styles will help you to recognise how best to present your proposal. Let us assume you can identify the types of information a person naturally responds to, and you have the flexibility to offer the same kind of information. Then you will be able to generate a feeling of understanding and enhance communication in a very powerful way regardless of subject matter. Like most of the techniques taught so far, the real convincer of just how influential this simple technique can be is using it yourself.

Everybody sorts their experiences in terms of what is important for them. We reveal our methods for coming to decisions as we speak and after half a dozen or so sentences they rapidly become clear to the careful listener. What we talk about, what we leave out, what we complain about. You can find out someone's decision-making strategy by asking simple questions and listening. Having established them, you then incorporate them in your presentation. You will be talking their language and have rapport, attention and interest.

Any open-ended question will uncover someone's natural inclinations for analysing information. The really clever questions are those which also elicit their buying strategy. How they make decisions and direct the client's mind towards owning what you are selling, for example, 'What exactly is it that you like about our products/services?'

C – The main ways of making decisions

Now let us look at the most common styles of how people make decisions. As we discuss these. they will start to fall into place as you identify people you know well, making their decisions in this way.

The 'moving towards' or 'moving away from' preference
'Moving towards' people are motivated by promotion, pay rises, a bigger house, car and so on. They are moving towards those objectives and things that they want to have. Anything you offer will stand a better chance of success if you show someone how it can help them towards their objectives.

Ask someone what motivates them and 'how' they answer will indicate if they have a clear direction in their motivation.

'Moving away from' people want to move away from things, usually problems. For example, one customer of mine is not so much motivated by what he can get as by what he can avoid. He clearly wishes to feel secure and will move away from the threat of losing his business. I presented my case to him in these terms, making him feel confident that he was not exposed to risk and that it would make him more secure and thus more away from the things he wishes to be at a distance from. He bought because I sold to him in a way that he could relate to and was motivated by.

The positive or negative preference

Most things can be stated in the positive or the negative. What we are looking for here is someone who predominantly phrases things in one or the other all the time. Again it is a strong indicator of how they come to decisions.

Many of course, are somewhere in between, and for them this decision-making category does not apply.

'How are you?' Fine.	or	Not too bad.
I want a keen price.	or	I do not want a high price.
I am overweight.	or	I am not my ideal weight.
I want delivery this week.	or	I do not want delivery after this week.
I want a good service.	or	I do not want a bad service.

The influence direction preference

When a prospective customer to your business is influenced in making a decision about what he thinks about you, there are four possible sources of influence:

- **Yourself.** How do you sound and look to him? What are his first impressions about you? What people has he known in the past that you remind him of?
- **Others.** What would those that he knows and trust make of you? Another manager or colleague, or perhaps mentally asking himself, if xxx was here right now, what opinion would they form?
- **Written and other material.** Your web page, e-mails, sales brochures, reviews, articles, testimonials, reviews, references etc.
- **A mixture of the above.**

In practice, I have found that one of the above patterns usually stands out clearly. If this is the case, it means that the influence direction is not important for them and should be ignored. If when weighing somebody up, you haven't decided in five minutes, you can safely ignore this category. This in itself is a valuable deletion.

The similarities or differences preference

'Similarities' deciders are constantly looking to compare any new information or communication with what they know. They match it up with something they are familiar with in order to judge it. When selling to someone like this you have to establish the favourable 'references' and make sure that you compare with these.

> For example, on a recruitment assignment I was working on, I noticed that the Managing Director (the client) constantly compared all the candidates to a previous employee he once employed. Clearly, I was going to win a placement when I came up with a candidate with a similar background and personality. So I continued questioning about this previous employee. I found someone (who did not incidentally fit the formal specification at all) and gave him a thorough briefing before the interview. He was offered and accepted the job at interview. Needless to say the candidate was also a similarities decider and this is one of the reasons why they got along so well.

'Differences' people are easily spotted as they respond with the opposite or exception to what you are saying. Often such people are thought of as being deliberately difficult. However, they are just running their 'decision-making programmes' in the only way they know how. That is how they process and learn. Recognise this and respond in kind. You will have no doubt if someone is a difference decider – it is very easy to recognise.

> For example, once while selling training seminars I recognised that my future client was a difference decider. So I changed my presentation and stressed the differences of my courses to alternatives. I was now speaking a language he understood easily and he was comfortable with what I was saying. Being on his frequency it was fairly straightforward from there to secure an order.

The general or specific preference

The generalist likes to look at the big picture in order to get a clear impression before making a decision. Price is rarely a major influence on these people. Showing potential overall payback will be a far more effective selling strategy. The entrepreneur Richard Branson is in this category.

Specific sorting people want all the details and scrutinise the figures with a fine-tooth comb. Your price will be looked at carefully in comparison to those of your competitors. This does not mean that specific deciders will choose the cheapest. In fact, they will analyse value for money of each alternative. Throughout a presentation, they will constantly be asking you questions requiring very precise detail. Do your homework thoroughly and you will get the deal.

The short-term or long-term preference

Those who are orientated to the future (see above) are often easily divided into short- or long-term thinkers. In the recruitment industry, this is a very valuable type of person. In considering a new candidate, does your client talk about what can be achieved in the next three months or three years? If three years, telling the changes that your candidate could achieve in the next three months won't get you far. Talk about long-term values, consistency, stability, seeing things through. A simple question such as *'What would you like the new candidate to achieve?'* will soon supply you with the information you need. They will of course be giving you far more information than they realise.

The task or relationship orientated preference

A very important category if you are looking for a job or trying to secure a brief as a recruiter. Ask, 'Tell me about the job itself?'. Observe the way the employer or prospective client answers.

The verb tenses

People using the past tense when you listen to them are always referring back. What happened back then as a good guide for the future is a typical belief that they would have. 'We tried it that way last year in our Southampton factory and found that it did not work,' might be a typical type of statement that you might hear.

Remember your Verbal Aikido skills, try a question such as, 'Has there ever been a time that you have done it this way and it was successful?'. With that question you are achieving two things. Firstly, you are matching his 'past deciding' style. Secondly, you are challenging the implied assumption in his statement that because it did not work last year means that it will not work now. The message here is obvious, if you have identified that someone makes decisions with reference to the past, tie your offer to his past successes. References and testimonials are very influential to these types of people as by indication they refer to the past. Past-oriented people invariably use the past tense of verbs, i.e. I thought, it was, we decided etc.

The present tense users. 'What I want to know is what can you do for me now?' The word 'now' used repeatedly is a good indicator of a present-time person. Telling this person what you have done for others in the past or the effect of accepting your offer in six months will be a waste of breath. Present-time people are spotted quickly because they invariably use the present tense of verbs, i.e. I think, am, decide etc.

The future tense users. 'What will it do for me?'. A 'future' person is always trying to get somewhere. Find out where that is and show him how you can help. Watch for frequent use of the future tense, i.e. I will, might, would etc.: *'I can see where this will lead.' 'I will give you an order if you will shave 10% off price.' 'I will give it some thought.'*

As you might have guessed, 'future people' tend also to be motivated more by moving towards 'good news' than distancing themselves from 'bad news'.

Notice the difference between *'I will ring you in three months to see what you think of the products'* and *'I will visit in three months, at that time we can look back at how the products have improved your general operations'*.

In our brains we code time. As you might imagine, the future for most people is hazy and uncertain whereas the past is clear and concrete. When you use the future tense therefore, the subconscious mind says 'maybe'. When you use the past tense, it is accepted by the subconscious mind.

The way to adapt this for your business is by projecting yourself into the future, looking back. Verb tenses also create interesting patterns that people use – the most common tense gives away how they think. I have noticed for example as a generalisation that British and American people, when asked the same question, will respond quite differently in this regard. British people tend to use the past tense much more and the Americans the future tense.

Other decision preferences

The above are the main categories of preference I have come across repeatedly. Very few people will not fit clearly into one of these. When you look for it, the preferred way of making decisions will appear obvious. The method of making decisions is formed very early on in life and becomes part of the basic 'software' of how people make sense of the world around them.

It will show up clearly in their general behaviour. Try to spot something in their language that keeps recurring. When you have this, you have the key that will unlock their decision-making style. Other patterns that I have come across are, money, numbers, places and people.

Progress now:

Think of someone you know for each of the categories above.

How can you use this knowledge in your sales calls?

Progress now:

Take three highlighter pens, green for future, red for past and blue for present. Now take something written by three different people in your industry and highlight each verb use appropriately. When you have done this, think about how you can use this knowledge to help your selling.

Now use other coloured pens and look for any other repeated patterns.

D – Developing your ability to sell to preferred decision styles

Once you have identified the decision-making method, then match your own approach and presentation to that method. It will obviously be easy, if not automatic, to match the decision-making methods that are similar or identical to your own. The real skill in persuasion is communicating in a pattern which is not yours, but that of the recipient of your communication.

Often, particularly at first, it will feel unnatural by definition. Making this effort is what I call customer service.

Many of my clients have told me that their staff seem to have great success with some clients whilst with others they don't seem to make any breakthroughs. Often the reason is that the successes are coming when they are talking to people with the same or similar ways of processing information as themselves. So I suggest before you start analysing what somebody else's decision-making methods are, find out what your own are. At the end of this chapter is an analysis sheet I have designed for this purpose. Ask your closest work and/or social colleagues to complete it for you.

Recognising and talking back to somebody in their preferred patterns is the quickest to learn and most practical sales technique that I have ever come across. It is also extremely powerful. I have personally observed individuals significantly increase their performance level by doing nothing more than concentrating on this technique.

The way to develop your skill at this technique is practice. It is best to practise in a controlled group with an experienced tutor. However, much learning can be gained by practising in your own group of at least three people and discussing the results. Put one person in 'the hot seat' and ask any open-ended question. Ask him or her to tell you about a favourite sport, recent holiday or whatever. Get him to talk for five minutes and record what he says. If he falters, ask more open-ended questions to keep him talking. With reference to the assessment sheet at the end of this chapter, each of you and your colleagues should assess what you think are the speaker's preferred styles for all the categories. Then put a circle around the three that you think are the most critical. If there are any categories that you are unsure of, ask a question that will give you that information.

When you are ready, ask the person to leave the room. Exchange notes with each other until you agree the three most crucial decision-making methods. Then choose a 'matcher' and a 'mismatcher'. The job of these two people is to make a two-minute presentation to the person and try to sell something. What you choose to sell is not important but it should be the same thing, for example a house, a car, a holiday, a boat or an insurance policy. It need not be related to what the person spoke about. Now ask the person back into the room. The 'matcher' goes first and makes his sales presentation using the three key decision preferences. Then the 'mismatcher' makes his presentation.

To illustrate, say the agreed three key methods are, Past, Generalising and Differences. The 'matcher' sells his product with reference to the past, tried and tested, etc, with generalisations as to the benefits and applications while stressing the differences. The 'mismatcher' talks in the future about what will happen in highly specific details, stressing the similarities. Afterwards, sit down and ask the person from whom he would buy. When you are in the 'hot seat' it will amaze you how much more appealing the matcher's presentation is. This is a vital experience because you will appreciate just how powerful this simple technique is and it will motivate you to become proficient at it. Your results in developing rapport and persuading will clearly increase.

Principal Preferences: Analysis Sheet
(Tick the decision-making method preferred)

1.	Moving towards	☐	12.	Task ☐
2.	Moving away		13.	Relationship ☐
3.	Positive	☐	14.	Short-term ☐
4.	Negative		15.	Long Term ☐
5.	Self	☐	16.	Past ☐
6.	Written		17.	Present ☐
7.	Others			
			18.	Future ☐
8.	Similarities	☐	19.	Money ☐
9.	Differences			
			20.	Numbers ☐
10.	Generalisations	☐	21.	Places ☐
11.	Specifics		22.	People ☐

E – Closing off

If after you have done all the above, the future client says something like, '*...well, let me think about it*', don't let them of the hook so easily. Behind this statement might be many things, such as they know they have not got the budget, or decision making authority, or more likely that somewhere in their mind is an objection that is casing them to pause. Probe for it – '*May I* *ask what exactly do you have to think about?'* You have done a lot of work to get this far, so don't be easily fobbed off now.

Sometimes they are just fearful of making a decision and you have to put your proposal in a way that makes it easy. Some people will put off all sorts of decisions and actions until they become critical. Sometimes you may find that a prospect is such hard work there are just easier fish to fry. Time management is always an important skill to master for entrepreneurs. You need to be constantly asking yourself if you are using your time at maximum effectiveness.

Progress now:

Selling has been described as the art of getting to yes. In fact, if you can get someone to repeatedly respond 'yes' irrespective of content, they will have formed the habit with you.

Call someone on the telephone and have a clock next to you that alarms in exactly five minutes. Tick a piece of paper each time you can get them to say the word, 'yes' in any context, content being irrelevant. Notice how you achieved this and then repeat the exercise on a different person.

I suggest that you ask yourself, at the start of each week, if you are continuing to rationalise and defend bad business decisions. We often do this because we have invested a certain amount of time and money and we need to get this back. In reality, any past money invested or profit spent is irrelevant to our current decision making. Admitting bad decisions and changing them is perhaps the best decision you can make. In selling if you put a lot of effort to into something that has not worked, learn the lessons and move on.

At the end of a conversation you need to seal everything up neatly. If this means a form to be signed, get it done then. Things left have a habit of being left for a very long time. You don't want to be playing chase up, after all your hard work and success.

Make sales, build businesses, have fun. Progress and prosper …

Appendix I

The Voice of Experience

'A wise man always learns, a wiser man lets wise men do the learning for him and heeds their advice.'

Alex McMillan

'Do not work for a limited company. Rise above the rest'

Royal Air Force Careers Advertisement

A – Learning from others

Experience is valuable when the lessons are learnt and behaviours and decision-making changed. Even better than this is to learn from the experience of others. Therefore I have included this section of extracts from carefully chosen interviews with successful entrepreneurs for their advice.

Wisdom comes with age and experience, but only if one chooses to learn from experiences. Otherwise we just repeat things. Many famous entrepreneurs went bust several times before making a great success. Some still went bust after making their fortune and then made another one. This shows that the real value of their enterprise was not in the tangible assets but in their skills developed through learning by their experiences. Ideas and knowledge are perhaps the key resources of any business.

Many entrepreneurs seem to have really hit success in their fifties or later, showing just how long their learning curve was. Yet they did not give up – they continued pursuing their dream. No doubt they had days when they felt like throwing in the towel. One of my objectives with this book is to accelerate your journey to increase sales in your enterprise by taking tips and advice from others.

People asking me for my advice are often interested in the initial transition from being a full time employee to getting their idea off the ground, and establishing a firm foundation from which to grow past breakeven to profitability. The following tips all come from successful entrepreneurs who have built a business or businesses to profitability. They share with us their secrets and lessons they learnt along the way. Progress, prosper and enjoy.

B – Words from the wise

Chris King is in his late forties and currently runs his own business in the telephone system industry (**www.kingmultimedia.com**). He has previously set up a new business, eventually selling it for a significant capital gain. He lives with is wife in the south of England.

Chris's advice:

1. Think about how happy you are with your present situation.
2. Go into something that you are proficient at.
3. Speak to and learn from people who have done it.
4. Sit down, write a plan and do it.
5. Get the finances right.
6. Know exactly what you want to achieve.
7. Get out there and do it.
8. Be willing to take risks, work hard and enjoy what you do.
9. In order to spot opportunities, be aware of your surroundings all the time by taking an interest in what people are doing. Look all the time for holes that need to be filled.
10. Rub shoulders with and study great people so as to improve yourself.

Vijay Dhir has started new enterprises, bought existing ones and made significant investments in property and shares. He is also a Justice of the Peace in his spare time. He is in his early fifties and lives with his wife and three children in their 18-acre home that he recently bought in Surrey.

Vijay's advice:

1. In your mind, you must be confident it is going to work.
2. Make informed decisions, do market research.
3. Watch the interest rate carefully if you borrow. Negotiate a clause for

an interest holiday just in case things go wrong.

4. Always be in a position to manoeuvre. A bank for example will want all your assets as security – don't do it. Just offer the item purchased or the business as security at most.

5. Start your own business as early as possible.

6. Be happy. The happiest people in life are those that have nothing. In India there are people that go off into the Himalayas to meditate – they are the happiest people I have ever seen.

7. Remember that success moves. It is like a bar of soap – you grab it and it moves away from you.

8. Always look for something that in money terms you can buy cheaper than what you can sell it for.

9. See potential not problems. Opportunity is always knocking on everyone's door but they can't see it and thus miss out.

10. Make it happen or move on, don't expect everything to work out.

Richard Baxter is joint founder and Managing Director of DCL Search and Selection (**richard.baxter@dclsearch.com**), which specialises in head-hunting senior IT professionals. Richard is in his thirties and lives with his wife and two children in South East London.

Richard's advice:

1. Identify you goals and write them down. Spend a maximum of 1% of your time writing them out and 99% going for them.

2. Get on with it quickly and get the money coming in.

3. The only financial measure worth monitoring is cash flow.

4. Look after your team and customers.

5. Trust your own judgement.

6. Never be afraid to change in the light of new results and information coming in.

7. Know your core values as a company and keep to them.

8. Do constant market research by asking people what they want.

9. Makes sure you have enough financial coverage, especially at the start.

10. Nothing in life goes entirely to plan – the important thing is fixing the problems when they arise.

C – Experience of Chris King

Chris: 'I made a decision to work for myself, so I started as a freelance consultant initially, working from home. I saw this as good experience in all the aspects of running a business. I rapidly became fully employed with orders still growing. I had to either turn the business away, or employ. I developed by using sub-contractors. This freed my time to develop the business.

Some people starting out believe that if they take a day off they are losing money. I think planning is essential which should include in your figures allowance for time off. I was successful and growing, yet becoming frustrated and felt I had to pursue a new enterprise. At the Ideal Home Exhibition, I was inspired by a new, at that time, themed telephone in the shape of a cartoon character. I rang BT to find the distributors and also talked to the importers who brought them in from the USA. I already had a profitable business so I was not under pressure and conducted thorough research and planned a business for retailing them in the UK. The bank and my wife thought I was crazy. I decided to open a shop with a partner.

It was clear that my partner and I had different motivations for the business and I bought his share out. I rented some suitable premises and stocked the shop with the phones and worked hard to get the enterprise off the ground. I then went to a different bank who backed us for taking on board a larger leasehold premises. BT then opened a major retail outlet – I was terrified. Yet, sales doubled! We grew because of their promoting the market for telephones. I learnt that one should never be afraid of competition, they all appeal to a slightly different type of customer and can help develop a market.

We also developed the business by going out and installing telephone systems and cabling, which was close to my original expertise. Things were going exceptionally well but I wanted to move on to other challenges. So I decided to sell the business. I clinched, or so I thought, a deal. The buyer cancelled two days before signing. I rang him and outlined all the benefits to him including the secure asset base if things should go wrong. I turned him around. I took my wife on a six months world tour from the profits!

Back in England, I was eager to get going again now armed with experience and success. I set up from home with low overheads and built a business quite quickly supporting 10 staff. I found that my biggest area of learning was in recruitment and people management. I learnt the hard way just how important people fitting in the team is. I then merged with a similar company and became the MD.

I believe that life is a terrific opportunity to improve yourself, providing you have your health, opportunities always keep coming up. I think fear stops many good potential entrepreneurs from having a go. This can be the fear of looking silly, being embarrassed, or not making the mortgage payments. Entrepreneurs have to be very self-disciplined.

You need to have an automatic positive mental attitude. I have found that competitors are not as bad for you as you might think and can sometimes be turned to advantage by for example establishing your market, partnerships etc. Success ultimately is about seeing the results of your plan happening and really enjoying your personal and business life. I strongly believe in ensuring you sleep, exercise, and eat well to provide the positive energy you need. So that when things go wrong, and they will, you can find out why, where and decide what can be done.'

D – Experience of Vijay Dhir

Vijay: 'My father was a Station Master in Africa and I came to England when I was 12 years old. Whilst doing my A levels I noticed commercial opportunities and pursued them. The first I noticed was that the local cinema was empty on Sunday mornings and there was a reasonable sized local Indian community. So I hired the time off the cinema owners and showed Indian films. I also set up an Indian grocery shop.

After school, I joined Plessey as an engineer, and enjoyed several promotions with up to 15 staff under my control. I needed something else though and I left and set up my own consultancy when I was 31. At this time I bought a launderette with living quarters above. The objective of this was to have my basic living expenses paid whilst I built up the consultancy. I always believe that in business it was best to not have all your eggs in the same basket. I thus target myself to make 2 out of 3 ventures successful and in making informed decisions by doing some research.

I can remember going to the bank for £500 to replace a washing machine for the launderette and being rejected. I was shocked, it was quite a lesson for me, how differently banks react to entrepreneurs than people in regular jobs. I then started talking to local restaurant owners and found an interest in having clean tablecloths delivered. I then bought some stock from a wholesaler and rented them out. Business was flourishing and I expanded with another launderette and a dry cleaners. I always bought the best quality at the cheapest price possible. I shop around until I am satisfied and negotiate strongly with everything that I buy or sell.

I then became interested in property investing, always looking for opportunities. I can remember in 1982 offering £18,000 for a property that was coming up at auction. The owner turned me down and I went to the auction to bid. Amazingly I secured it for £14,000. I sold it six months later for £26,000. I later came across a 3-bedroom property value at £120,000, which I bought for £75,000. The owner was leaving the country permanently and wanted to get rid of it for a quick decision and deal.

If you don't take risks, it is very difficult to be successful. You cannot think all the time if you can sell it or not. You have to decide that you are going to sell it and just do it.

In 1987, I bought a large property with a view to developing it in to a residential nursing care home. It was an empty house valued at £1.25 million on offer for £800,000. That was a big risk. Interest rates were high and rising. The launderettes were supporting it but not enough. I had to sell all my properties, shares and businesses. We had a breakeven point at 19 residents and we still were clearly not going to continue to make ends meet. I needed five more people. We contacted every hospital and person we could think of. I find in desperation you can achieve anything. I have three sayings. There is no knowledge without college, no life without wife and no gain without pain. You must try things and get feedback until you know what works. It took me five years in business to accumulate a £100,000 and a couple of years more to make my first million. I strongly believe in being a sole trader, partnerships are risky and tend to work best when the partners are equal.'

E – Experience of Richard Baxter

Richard: 'My first exposure to business was as a child, when I lived above my father's café. My first real job though after school was selling insurance. I later moved to an IT recruitment company. I was very happy there, successful and spent five years working for a boss I respected, until a recession hit and he sold out. The new owners were going for floatation and were focused on an advertising approach. I believed that there was a need and an opportunity in the market for a headhunting based operation. I knew this method could fill more jobs with more appropriate people, in a shorter time for less money. I had a strong conviction and passion in this and decided to launch DCL Search and Selection.

I was the controlling shareholder and had two partners, one who I later bought out. We set up in a flat, installed telephone lines and bought a second hand PC. Our sole objective was to make money and prove to ourselves that we could run a profitable business. We achieved a profit in our first year. Our next goal was to take on board an office and build a profitable team of 10-12 recruiters.

Our next growth stage was to move the contingency base of our business to a retained one. This means that we were paid up front to take on a headhunting assignment. We gave guarantees and a fully professional service. In fact demand was high for a quality service and we soon became 100% retained and all assignments were filled through headhunting.

Currently we have reintroduced contingency recruitment but really only as an easy way to open doors to win respect for our service and gain longer term retained clients. I spend most of my personal time making high-level sales presentations, listening to people's needs and explaining what we can offer. Our current goal is to reach 50 staff with £50million turnover with 50% profitability. Then we intend to expand internationally in the English speaking world.'

Progress and prosper ...

Appendix 2

Daily Motivation

Ten-minute daily booster

The most important ingredient to selling your products and services is you!

If you are feeling uplifted, in a great mood and motivated, most people you talk to will be interested in your proposal, assuming it has commercial viability. Add this to the techniques in this book and you will have all that you need.

So in this appendix, I give you a very simple tool that you can use every day, on the train to work, or whilst you have your morning coffee. It will only take ten minutes. The nature of the exercise will be different every day, for reasons you will understand soon.

I call the exercise, *Energy Injection*, for that is what it does, – guaranteed. I will briefly explain why it works.

Each word we hear is represented in some way in our mind. Internal pictures, sounds no doubt related and coming from previous experiences. This therefore produces a certain feeling. Obviously positive words produce positive images and sounds. These in turn trigger associated feelings. Negative the opposite. So the trick is to force ourselves to get into the habit of hearing positive words, to fire us up to produce results. Negative ones can also be used usefully by motivating us to avoid those feelings. Most of the words we hear in a day are not from other people, but from our own internal voices. This exercise will thus set you up nicely for the day – the effects will last 24 hours.

Below is a list of positive words.

Every day pick half a dozen of them. You can work down the list or pick them at will. You only have to make up and speak the word internally. Do so in the most upbeat tone, one that suggests the word itself.

For each word:

1. Make up a motivational sentence that has this word in it.
2. Describe something in your life using this word.
3. Decide a goal-oriented action you can do today related in some way to this word.
4. Make a promise to yourself about what you will do today, using this word.
5. After you have done the above for six words write down three goals that you would and could realistically achieve by tonight.
6. Think of three negative feelings and name them, that you would feel tonight if you let yourself down on today's goals.
7. Name two long-term negative consequences if you do not achieve today's goals.

Abundant	Accelerate	Achieve	Action
Advance	Adventure	Alert	Alive
Amaze	Arouse	Astonish	Astound
Awaken	Awesome	Beautiful	Bliss
Bountiful	Brainwave	Breakthrough	Brilliant
Bubbly	Confident	Create	Decisive
Delight	Determined	Development	Discover
Dream	Dynamic	Empower	Energise
Enjoy	Enliven	Enthral	Enthusiasm
Euphoric	Exceptional	Exciting	Extraordinary
Fabulous	Fantastic	Fascination	Favourite
Fire up	First	Flourish	Flow
Focus	Freedom	Fresh	Fruitful
Galore	Glitter	Glorious	Glow
Great	Growth	Happy	High-powered
Incredible	Inspire	Invest	Invigorate
Joy	Leadership	Leap	Leverage

Lively	Love	Luxury	Magnificent
Miracle	Momentum	Motivated	Opportunity
Paradise	Passion	Peak	Plentiful
Positive	Power	Profit	Progress
Propose	Prosper	Radiant	Radiate
Ravish	Relish	Revel	Rich
Shine	Sing	Smile	Sparkle
Special	Strength	Spirit	Stimulate
Success	Sunshine	Superior	Superstar
Sweeten	Synergy	Terrific	Thrill
Thrive	Tremendous	Vibrant	Vigour
Vitality	Vivid	Warmth	Wealth
Winner	Wonderful	Yes	Zest

Example:

Chosen word : Abundant

1. There are abundant opportunities for me to sell my services.
2. My ideas to push myself forward are in abundance.
3. Today I will call on the phone until I get a new sales lead. They are out there in abundance I just have to keep sifting.
4. I will believe that people with money to spend are in abundance.

Three goals for today:

5. Bring in one new client.
6. Make those calls I have been putting off.
7. Write a quality e-mail signature.

Negative feelings:

8. Disappointed in myself for not having completed my day goals and be one step ahead.

9. Frustrated that I am still working on what I want to do rather than priorities.
10. Worried that I am losing business unnecessarily.

Long-term consequence:

11. I will trade at a loss if I do not get new clients in.
12. I will still have to worry about the mortgage and other loans.

When you have done the above make a decision to do all that you can do to avoid those bad feelings tonight. Control you destiny.

Your turn – just work through the following:

Pick a word from the above list:

Sentences using this word are:

1.

2.

3.

4.

Three goals for today:

5.

6.

7.

Negative feelings:

8.

9.

10.

Long-term consequence:

11.

12.

Remember to smile.

Have a fantastic day.

Progress and Prosper...

Useful websites

www.alexmcmillan.com
www.startups.co.uk (magazine)
www.businesslink.org
www.fsb.org.uk   (Federation of Small Businesses)
www.britishchambers.org.uk
www.smallbusinessadvice.org.uk
www.bvca.co.uk   (British Venture Capital Association)
www.seminarworld.co.uk (focuses on SMEs)
www.avondale-group.co.uk (business consulting for entrepreneurs)
www.entrepreneur.com
www.richdad.com
www.richardbandler.com (founder of NLP)
www.paulmckenna.com (NLP UK training site)

Bibliography

Awaken The Giant Within, Anthony Robbins, Simon and Schuster, 1992.

Beliefs, Robert Dilts, Tim Hallbom and Suzy Smith, Metamorphous Press, 1994.

Beyond Selling, Dan Bagley and Ed Reese, Meta Publications, 1987.

Be Your Own Brand David McNally & Karl D. Speak, Berrett-Kephler Inc, 2002

Change Your Mind – And Keep The Change, Steve and Connirae Andreas, Real People Press, 1987.

Changing Belief Systems With NLP, Robert Dilts, Meta Publications, 1990

Coach (Be a Better and Beyond Series), Steve Banister and Amanda Vickers, Hodder and Stoughton, 2003

Entrepreneur (Be a Better and Beyond Series) Alex McMillan, Hodder & Stoughton, 2003

Frogs Into Princes, Richard Bandler and John Grinder, Real People Press, 1979.

Getting Everything You Can Get Out Of All That You've Got. Jay Abraham Judy Piatkus Ltd, 2000

How to Buy and Sell a Business for Capital Wealth. Kevin Uphill and Alex McMillan Publisher to be advised.

Influencing With Integrity, Genie Z. Laborde, Syntony Publishing, 1987.

Introducing Neuro-Linguistic Programming, John Seymour and Joseph O'Connor, Harper Collins, 1993.

Magic In Action, Richard Bandler, Real People Press, 1984.

Motivator (Be a Better and Beyond series), Frances Coombes, Hodder and Stoughton, 2003

Modern Persuasion Strategies: The Hidden Advantage In Selling, DJ Moine and JH Herd, Metamorphous Press, 1980.

Patterns Of Hypnotic Techniques Of Milton H Erickson MD Vol 1, Richard Bandler and John Grinder, Meta Publications, 1977.

Patterns Of Hypnotic Techniques Of Milton H Erickson MD Vol 2, Richard Bandler, John Grinder and Judith DeLozier, Meta Publications, 1977.

Practical Magic, Stephen Lankton, Meta Publications, 1979.

Precision, Michael McMaster and John Grinder, Metamorphous Press, 1980.

Reframing, Richard Bandler and John Grinder, Real People Press, 1982.

Results On Target, Bruce Dilman, Outcome Publications, 1989.

Self-Promotion for the Creative Person. Lee Silber, Three Rivers Press, 2001

Selling With NLP, Kerry Johnson, Nicholas Brierley Publishing, 1994.

The Emprint Method, Leslie Cameron-Bandler, David Gordon and Michael Lebeau, Future Pace, 1985.

The Structure Of Magic Vol 1, Richard Bandler and John Grinder, Science and Behaviour Books, 1975.

The Structure Of Magic Vol 2, Richard Bandler and John Grinder, Science and Behaviour Books, 1975.
Time For A Change, Richard Bandler, Meta Publications, 1994.

Unlimited Power, Anthony Robbins, Simon and Schuster, 1990.

Using Your Brain For A Change, Richard Bandler, Real People Press, 1981.

Your First Year In Network Marketing, Mark Yarnell, Rene Reid Yarnell, Prima Publishing 1998

Your Ticket To Success, Alex McMillan, Management Books 2000, 1996

Index

Thank you for reading this book
I know that you are about to benefit from it.

To view my latest products, services, webinars, latest tips for
entrepreneurs and much more please visit **www.alexmcmillan.com**

Alex McMillan
Business Speaker/Motivator/Coach

Alex is an expert authority on raising and
maintaining motivation so as to achieve
consistent results and build businesses.
His programmes motivate and inspire
whilst giving practical tips and techniques
that can be applied immediately
afterwards.
Participants always enjoy his high-energy,
high-impact presentations and workshops,
which get straight to the point.

Topics include:

Motivation, Selling, Entrepreneurship, Making Easy Money in What Others
See As A Tough Market, Going for Growth, NLP Applied to Selling,
Consistent Top Billing For Recruitment Consultants.

Programs include:

- Harnessing the Power of Negative Thinking
- The 100K Club
- Manager Magic
- Entrepreneur – The Money Magnet
- Peak Performance Selling

Available as a one to one performance coach for the very ambitious.

Short Presentations / Audio CDs:

- Advanced selling for beginners.
- How to make money through your own business.
- How to be a top earning recruitment consultant.
- How to win your dream job.
- How to earn over 100K in sales

Reviews

'*Reading up to chapter 5 has led me to re-evaluate my attitudes as to how I carry out my business activities. As a result, I have confidently embarked on a new business venture whilst at the same time, I am rebuilding my existing businesses.*

I am having such an exciting time now, in a way, I don't want to know what comes next in the book. It might say something like "don't do too much at once". Nevertheless, I shall endeavour to finish it.

Many thanks for a truly enlightening read.'

Carl Adamson, Business Owner, **www.Webnical.com**

'*In an increasingly complex world, the differentiators and benefits between one product and another are hard to determine. This means the decision to buy is increasingly influenced on an emotional level by the brand and the people selling the product. Essentially, this means people buy people. This exciting book shows you in easy steps how to make sure it is you they buy. It is invaluable.*'

Kevin Uphill, MD, **www.avondale-group.co.uk**

'*This concise guide is full of inspirational and empowering advice that really gets to the core of personal sales effectiveness. Combines pragmatic, easy to understand sales concepts and techniques with a powerful insight into the behavioural and psychological elements that drive business success. Anyone wishing to achieve new heights in performance should certainly work through the simple yet searching exercises – definitely the first step in the journey to fulfill your true potential.*'

David Leyshon, MD, Butler International, **www.uk.butler.com**

'*A must have book for any new business that wants to grow fast.*'

Marcus Austin, Ed-in-chief , **Startups.co.uk**